THE NEW RULES OF ENTREPRENEURSHIP

WHAT IT REALLY TAKES TO BECOME A SAVVY AND SUCCESSFUL ENTREPRENEUR

Rob Yeung

Marshall Cavendish
Business

This book was previously published as *Entrepreneurship: The New Rules*
Copyright © 2011 Rob Yeung
Cover design: Jim Banting

Published in 2011 by Marshall Cavendish Business
An imprint of Marshall Cavendish International

PO Box 65829, London EC1P 1NY, United Kingdom
info@marshallcavendish.co.uk

and

1 New Industrial Road, Singapore 536196
genrefsales@sg.marshallcavendish.com
www.marshallcavendish.com/genref

Other Marshall Cavendish offices: Marshall Cavendish Corporation. 99 White Plains
Road, Tarrytown NY 10591-9001, USA • Marshall Cavendish International (Thailand)
Co Ltd. 253 Asoke, 12th Flr, Sukhumvit 21 Road, Klongtoey Nua, Wattana, Bangkok
10110, Thailand • Marshall Cavendish (Malaysia) Sdn Bhd. Times Subang, Lot 46,
Subang Hi-Tech Industrial Park, Batu Tiga, 40000 Shah Alam, Selangor Darul Ehsan,
Malaysia

Marshall Cavendish is a trademark of Times Publishing Limited

The right of Rob Yeung to be identified as the author of this work has been asserted by
him in accordance with the Copyright, Designs and Patents Act 1988.

A CIP record for this book is available from the British Library

ISBN 978-981-4351-02-7

Printed in Singapore by Fabulous Printers Pte Ltd

Contents

Foreword

Come on, admit it. The idea of becoming an entrepreneur and becoming your own boss is cool. Perhaps you want to strike out in a new direction and make your first million. Maybe you wish you could do it or maybe already are doing it.

Whatever your situation, *Entrepreneurship: The New Rules* is your guidebook for getting it right.

This book looks at moving outside of the corporate hierarchy and doing your own thing. Any ordinary person can become an entrepreneur. Yes, you read that correctly. Entrepreneurship isn't about experience or special training. It's about using your brain, motivating yourself, and building relationships with the right people. So, yes, anyone can do it.

You could become self-employed, set up a partnership, invest in a franchise, buy a business, build an empire, invent a new gadget, or launch a new service. You could work from home or lease an office, set up a website or showroom, work on your own or in a team of 20. You could set up a tiny outfit to target a niche market or a giant company to sell to the masses. Entrepreneurship is about any or all of these things, and more.

I've had the pleasure of working with top business-people and entrepreneurs in companies large and small. In the last few years, I've had the pleasure (and pain) of growing my own consultancy too, so much of what I advise I know from first-hand experience.

There are plenty of books that take you through the practical aspects of setting up your own venture – from opening a business bank account and tracking your finances to chasing customers for payment and calculating your tax bills – but this book isn't one of them. Businesses don't succeed or fail based on whether you pick the right bank account. Don't sweat the small stuff. I want you to think much bigger than that.

This book is about the spirit of entrepreneurship – the stuff that truly distinguishes successful entrepreneurs from wannabes and failures. Look at famous entrepreneurs in the world today. Icons such as Michael Dell, Donald Trump, Richard Branson, and Li Ka Shing grew their businesses by identifying opportunities and persisting in the face of adversity, selling ideas and brokering deals, inspiring their employees and engaging their customers. Business is fundamentally about people – your mental toughness and ability to build relationships with others. Let's focus on the stuff that matters: the mindset and way of thinking, and let's help you succeed.

Perhaps you don't yet have an idea for a business but know that you want to strike out on your own. That's OK, this book can help you find the right concept for your business. Maybe you have the seed of an idea but don't know how to grow it into a full-blown business, or you have already taken some initial steps but want to take it to the next stage. You might even be a thriving entrepreneur, but realize that the competition is tough and want to become a better one. Whatever your situation, this book will help you to raise your game and become a self-made entrepreneur.

Do drop me an email to let me know how you get on. Work hard and succeed well!

Rob Yeung
rob@talentspace.co.uk

Introduction

Want to experience the thrill of being your own boss? Want to put your talents to good use and throw off the shackles of corporate life?

That's great if you do – tens of thousands of people do it every year and never look back.

Entrepreneurs come in all shapes and sizes. While a few offer breathtakingly amazing innovations, many thrive simply by offering variations on well-established themes. They aren't just shipping magnates, empire builders, hi-tech geniuses and internet wizards. They are also everything from consultants and freelance workers to lawyers, accountants, restaurateurs, designers, acupuncturists, hairdressers, agents, investors, engineers, retailers, and builders. They offer their products and services from shops, offices, salons, spare bedrooms, showrooms, websites, hotels, clinics, workshops, restaurants, retail outlets, the list goes on.

Then there are the reasons that people become entrepreneurs. A few fall into it by accident after losing their job or getting fed up of corporate life. Some want to turn their passion or hobby into the focus of their work. Many have audacious goals to grow businesses that will make them rich. Others want to turn clever ideas or inventions into new products, services, or processes. Then there are those who set up on their own for lifestyle reasons, wanting to take control of their work–life balance and claim their personal lives back.

Some entrepreneurs start with practically no budget at their disposal, having enough money only to cover their costs at the local photocopy shop or internet café. Others secure venture capital backing and have millions to launch their wares upon the world.

There isn't a template for what kind of people become successful entrepreneurs – they are men and women, university graduates as well as school drop-outs, mildly dyslexic, experienced managers as well as naive but enthusiastic moguls in the making.

It's true – anyone can become a successful entrepreneur. That much should be clear. Becoming your own boss and succeeding in business isn't about being good with balance sheets and spreadsheets. Those are the mere tools of businesspeople. What makes a business succeed are passion and determination, relationship-building skills and hard work. As long as you genuinely want to succeed, you will.

Disregard the hype about entrepreneurs

Entrepreneurs are special people, right?

Wrong.

The media loves to portray entrepreneurs as being distinctive individuals, mavericks set apart from the rest of humanity. The business media like nothing more than telling the tale of the entrepreneur who has succeeded from an early age. Of the child who sells cold drinks at school on a hot day or the enterprising youngster who baked cakes and sold them to their friends' parents or the aspiring kid who set up an organized crime syndicate and struck fear into the city's police at the age of seven. OK, so maybe I haven't read about that last one.

All of those are just good stories and stories are sometimes as removed from reality as fables. The media are there to tell stories and sell papers – and the story of an ordinary person who had a decent, but perhaps uneventful, upbringing and education doesn't make for a dramatic tale. Or you may have read about entrepreneurs who were so streetwise and savvy that they dropped out of school or university to turn their dreams into gold. Perhaps you've read a biography or two of high-profile entrepreneurs and marveled at their thrusting, pushy nature and way with words. Those are only sagas spun to sell magazines, newspapers, and books too.

For every pushy and extrovert entrepreneur, there are probably a half-dozen equally successful, quieter entrepreneurs who shun the media spotlight and prefer to get on with the job of making their businesses a success.

Sadly, too many people believe the nonsense that you need to be special. So please believe me when I say that you don't need to be a certain type of person. You don't need to have had an extraordinary upbringing. As long as you can come up with a good idea that you can get passionate about and are prepared to commit totally to turning into a commercial enterprise, you can be a successful entrepreneur.

Invest in perspiration, not education

Thousands of people every year stump up huge fees to attend business schools and, for the most part, their goals are to graduate and become entrepreneurs – to start up businesses, get venture capitalists to invest tens of millions, and become obscenely rich and successful.

You don't need to have been to business school or to have studied business because business courses only teach you what has worked in the past. Sure, they can give you a solid grounding on how to deal with the finances and understand how businesses tend to market and sell, recruit and manage. What they end up doing though is teaching people about ways in which business should and should not be done.

Entrepreneurs, on the other hand, often try to do something new, different, better. To use the cliché, entrepreneurship is sometimes about "thinking outside of the box." Without a formal business education, you won't need to think outside of the box because you were never taught to think inside of it. You might end up challenging a status quo or subverting an industry assumption that others have been educated to accept.

If you have spent years at business school, celebrate it

and use those lessons in how businesses are run to make sure you don't make the mistakes of businesses of the past. If you haven't been to business school, celebrate that too because your open-mindedness might just allow you to ask the "stupid question" that no one else would ever dare ask, and that might just be the perfect starting point for making your business a success.

Do something new or tackle something old

What kind of businesses does the word entrepreneur summon up in your mind? There's sometimes a perception that you can only be an entrepreneur if you do something innovative, groundbreaking, entirely different; that you must come up with a brainwave so unique that others will pinch themselves for not having thought of it first. However, that only encapsulates a tiny minority of entrepreneurs. In fact, ideas that are too radical can often fail because customers, suppliers, and investors may be too confused or bemused by them.

Rather than creating something completely new, many entrepreneurs merely tweak what already exists or offer their own version of it.

Take the retailers, restaurant groups, and launderette chains on your own high street. Consider the firms of accountants, web designers, plumbers, and solicitors in your local business directory. Every one of them was started by an entrepreneur. None of them are trying to invent a replacement for the combustion engine or provide a solution to poverty in the developing world.

Of course the successful entrepreneurs offer novel variations on a theme. In recent years, I've come across successful businesses launching on very simple concepts. A "green" taxi car service operating only environmentally friendly hybrid cars. A chain of suburban hairdressing salons offering top-class hair cuts to customers who can't be bothered to venture into the city center. A company using software engineers based in Bangalore in India to slash the costs of designing a website by two-thirds.

Maybe your twist could be better customer service, quality, or speed, or taking a product to a different customer group that is as yet under-appreciated by others. For your venture, perhaps doing something slightly differently but just better than anyone else could be all you need.

Count yourself in

Still don't believe me that anyone can do it?

Well, these numbers should provide the proof you need.

In the UK, there are over 3 million small businesses with no employees (i.e. they consist only of one person – the owner). These 3 million businesses had a combined turnover of nearly £200 billion. In the US, there are 17 million small businesses with just one or two employees (again, including the owner), generating a staggering trillion dollars in revenues a year. That's a lot of people and a lot of money.

In the UK alone, around 200,000 people decided to start up their own businesses in the last year. Perhaps this year you will be among the many hundreds of thousands worldwide who will quit their jobs and turn themselves into mini-moguls and budding tycoons.

Now really is the time to sack the boss and do your own thing.

01

Thinking Like An Entrepreneur

First the bad news; you can't just flick a switch that says "become an entrepreneur" and expect an easy life, success, riches, and recognition to come your way. It takes hard work and you will work long hours.

However, the first step toward becoming an entrepreneur requires no action at all. It is not about acting, but thinking. You need to prepare yourself for the entrepreneurial journey by learning to think like one:

- To understand that you must have a passion for what you do and enjoy the business of being in business.
- To retrain your brain to get used to the sometimes uncertain life of being your own boss.
- To realize that you need to make mistakes to learn what works and what doesn't.

Chase a passion, not cash
Have a passion and you will make money. Want only to make money and you won't.

It's pretty simple, really.

Wanting to be rich does not generate wealth. Yes, some entrepreneurs create huge business empires and become vastly rich, but even when they make their millions they carry on working regardless. They are not driven by money, but the love of what they do. They are often gripped by an almost desperate determination to make their mark and do something better.

Think about it. If you don't genuinely enjoy or even love what you do, how will you motivate yourself? If you have to write that proposal, are you going to be thinking "oh no, not that damn document!" or "I can't wait to tell the world about my idea!"? If you need to give a pitch about your business, will you be scrabbling around for ways to pad out your presentation or bubbling over with too many ideas?

True entrepreneurs have discovered that if they have a passion and manage to communicate it to their customers, the money comes almost as an afterthought. Business people who do it purely for the money aren't true entrepreneurs. Greed is not the same as passion, and without that passion and enthusiasm to deliver something new or better, these people run out of energy and flee back to comfortable jobs working for someone else.

Don't let that be you. Whatever you choose to do in your business, make sure you can get excited about it. If you don't, how can you expect your customers to do so?

Enjoy business and people

So passion is top of that checklist of requirements for becoming an entrepreneur but it's not enough. Before you throw your job in your boss's face, consider next whether you have an enthusiasm for the idea of running a business. Of striking deals with suppliers. Of poring over spreadsheets and managing cash and watching profit. Of handling technology problems, invoicing snags and customer complaints. And that's just the start of it.

Do those thoughts excite you or horrify you?

But there's more to it than just enjoying the world of business.

Probably of more importance is having an appetite for engaging with other people. This is because entrepreneurship is fundamentally about people and relationships. It's about forging social connections with investors, suppliers, employees, customers, and even competitors.

Even if you have the best business plan in the world, investors are only going to stump up funds if they trust you to deliver on your plan. Suppliers need to understand your vision. Employees might need some persuading to join your little outfit rather than some more established firm. It goes without saying that customers are going to need some more convincing to buy your products or services. In addition, it wouldn't hurt to have friendly relationships with competitors to understand industry trends too.

If all of that communicating and negotiating, and influencing and persuading sounds like your idea of hell, then entrepreneurship is not for you. Consider that you might be better suited to settling into a more comfortable, perhaps employed existence. Avoid having to get your hands dirty with the horrible responsibility of financial goings-on and business decisions, and dealing with people on a daily basis.

If that still hasn't put you off, read on.

Take responsibility

From wage slave to thrusting tycoon, your first step is to adjust the way you think about your work and life. With that shift in mindset will come changes in how you behave and live your life from now on too.

Corporate life can get terribly comfortable and predictable. Wage slaves (or employees, as they are more politely known) get used to having a regular income. They have regular hours. They have a clear role and colleagues who can support them. You might have had a sales team to find customers, an accounts team to chase them for money. Maybe you had a secretary to handle your administration or a team of lackeys to do stuff that you were too important to sully yourself with.

As an entrepreneur, all of that has to go. So long, farewell, auf wiedersehen, goodbye. Your income will become irregular. From now on, if you don't earn, you don't eat. Your hours will fluctuate from almost nothing in a quiet week to every hour you aren't sleeping when necessary. Suddenly your clear role will be replaced by a need to do everything and anything. Not a single customer will come your way unless you pursue them, engage with them, persuade them to give you a chance. Customers won't pay unless you send them a bill. If you need to send a fax or write a proposal, you can't pass it on to your secretary or a junior member of the team – it'll be you who needs to figure out the fax machine or sit at your desk into the night.

Of course, entrepreneurs love it. They love the freedom and opportunity to carve out their own careers rather than merely do what they are told to do. It does, though, take getting used to.

Just thought I would warn you!

Enjoy making mistakes

Wages slaves are instructed not to make mistakes; entrepreneurs thrive on them.

I've heard some entrepreneurs say that you aren't a real entrepreneur until you have seen at least one business go bust. Personally, I wouldn't go that far but my point is that you have to be willing to make mistakes. To try new ways of working and understand what doesn't work. To go wrong publicly and occasionally have people snigger or shake their heads at you.

Too many would-be entrepreneurs allow themselves to be held back by their own fear of failure. They don't want to go wrong and look foolish or stupid. They worry what others might think. They look for approval and, when others tell them that their idea won't work, they stall and chew their fingernails, and wonder what to do next. That procrastination is often enough for the opportunity to slip them by, for someone else with a similar idea to have the guts to trial and test it and bring it to market.

I can pretty much guarantee you that your idea won't work. At least, not at first. Not in the way you first intend it. However, each of your mistakes is an opportunity to learn, to improve your process, and eliminate methods that don't work. Each one is an experiment that will help you find the right formula. You will only find the right path when you have gone down lots of blind avenues, made lots of faltering errors, and bungled a handful of attempts.

Entrepreneurs get it wrong but are determined enough to carry on regardless. They work at their ideas and they adjust their goals constantly in the light of new information on what competitors are doing, what customers are asking for, and what the technology allows them to do.

The message is simple. Be ready to make mistakes – lots of them. Give yourself a pat on the back every time something doesn't work, because your mistakes will ultimately allow you to figure out how to succeed.

Commit to getting started

It doesn't matter how you get started as long as you do.

Reading this book and then setting it aside is not the aim of the book. If I can persuade you to spend just an hour with pen and paper jotting some ideas down, that's a start. A great start, in fact. There are too many people who merely wish they could be entrepreneurs. They imagine what it would be like to run their own businesses. They dream and talk about wanting to become entrepreneurs but, behind the words, there are no actions to make it happen; they find it easier to come up with excuses for not doing it and delude themselves that they are going to do it "soon."

That first hour of work and then another and then another will set you aside from the majority of those wannabes who never do anything about it. A handful of hours is all it takes – at least at first. Not everyone can quit their jobs and throw all of their energies into a new venture. Many successful entrepreneurs started out fairly cautiously, by working on their new venture part-time while juggling the regular income of their full-time occupation. There is no reason you couldn't do that to begin with.

Whatever you do, don't let yourself become one of those spectators who merely watch and wish it could be them. Make sure you set that time aside to think, discuss, plan, or research without letting tiredness or work commitments or family engagements or laziness get in your way.

Just a few hours a week – is that too much to ask of yourself?

02

Nurturing Your Ideas

So what's your new business going to do?

What? You don't know?

Well, the good news is that you don't need to know.

Many entrepreneurs decide only that they want to work for themselves. They start with a blank sheet of paper and look around for that fresh angle on an old idea or a new twist on an existing one. With a bitof research, talking to people, and going online, they find the idea that works for them. Maybe a way to tweak someone else's idea, modify a product that already exists, or offer a service packaged up in a slightly different way. A few of them even manage to come up with that pulse-pounding, earth-shattering, rule-breaking idea.

Let's move on to the next phase of the entrepreneurial journey by helping you to find a way to imagine something new, different, better.

Ponder, reflect, and contemplate

One way of building a business is to look to your own talents. If you can do something with ease that others find difficult, you might be able to build a business on it. Don't discount your talents just because you find they come naturally to you. I know someone who is a gifted classical scholar; he handles Latin and Ancient Greek as easily as the rest of us count one, two, three. He has managed to turn his gift into a children's tutoring service that has grown 100 percent in the last year and will grow another 100 percent this year.

Remember that you have to be passionate about what you want to do, or at least excited by it. If someone offered to triple my salary to renovate old houses, I couldn't do it. For me to strip wallpaper and knock down walls, and plaster and paint and – well, I just couldn't bear the thought. If you can't stand computers, don't get into software solutions, no matter how profitable the idea could be. If you don't like lots of customers asking stupid questions, don't go into retail.

What do you do well? Perhaps you are a whiz with technology or a natural sales person. Maybe you have an analytical brain or are good at coaching other people. Or, deep down, maybe you love antiques or have a passion for fashion.

As you ponder, reflect, and contemplate on what kind of a business to build, make sure that your business idea matches your temperament.

Investigate new markets, niches, and opportunities

Another way to look for a winning business concept is to steal ideas from elsewhere. Don't worry, you're not going to be stealing anything literally. In business, appropriating someone else's idea is usually called "best practice sharing" or "benchmarking." Business-people do it all the time; copying the best of what someone else does, but trying to make it better.

One way to steal without anyone noticing is to look abroad for inspiration. Find an idea that has worked in another country and transfer it home. Entrepreneurs set up the Coffee Republic chain in the UK after having seen upmarket coffee shops in New York City. And Chinese e-commerce company Alibaba took their idea from eBay USA in setting up their own auction site Taobao.

Or, reversing the logic, could there be an opportunity to export a product or service from home to some country elsewhere?

Entrepreneurs can jump on ideas that big companies can't or won't respond to. Maybe a big company feels an idea is too risky or would require too much upheaval and change to respond to. Or a big company might decide that the market isn't big enough for it to enter. What is too small for a big company might still be plenty large enough for you. Look at the ideas the big businesses in your sector reject or fail at and see if you can do it on a niche scale.

It doesn't matter if you don't know anything about organic baby food or clothing design for Muslim women. You can always learn or find someone who does. As long as you can come up with a concept that you can get excited about, that's good enough for now.

Pick up on market trends

The only thing that stays constant is change. The world,

people, and society are changing. The children of today experience problems and opportunities that we never had, and we will experience old age in a different way from our parents.

Look at the world around you and tap into how work and home life and communities are changing. With change come shifting lifestyles, needs, and opportunities.

I see a trend for people to want to know what they're eating – they want fresh, locally farmed, perhaps organic produce as opposed to packaged food stuffed with preservatives and hydrogenated fat. People are more worried about getting fat but don't know how (or can't really be bothered) to get fitter and thinner.

Perhaps in a related vein, I see people waking up to notions such as climate change, environmental impact, and ethical trade. Even big businesses are getting in on the act of "corporate social responsibility."

I see people working longer hours and becoming increasingly "cash rich, but time poor." They want more convenience from their products and services – in everything from having to cook less to having someone else do their ironing for them. At the same time, more and more workers want to be their own bosses rather than spending their lives working for others.

Perhaps because they are working longer hours, I see consumers wanting to buy products and services that are unique and luxurious. Mass retailers are fighting to offer limited editions and personalized services and products to tempt consumers to spend, spend, spend.

People want to travel the world more too, but to do so in an authentic fashion – wanting to experience less the tourist's version of a country and more of what the locals live and breathe on a daily basis. At the same time, they crave ways to safeguard themselves against threats such as terrorism and global disease pandemics.

From the dissolution of the traditional family to increasing numbers of the elderly as the population continues to age, I see the make-up of the population shifting. Minority groups of all sorts continue to grow in numbers too. Each of these presents opportunities to entrepreneurs willing to service their individual needs.

I haven't even started on the impact of technology on our lives – of opportunities on the internet and mobile phones, and gadgets that simplify our lives and allow us to have more fun on the move.

And those are just the trends that I can think of without having to really put my mind to it. What other trends – and opportunities – could you plug into?

Broaden your perspective

This may sound insane, but what would happen if you could buy eggs in a cone-shaped box? What if the food in a restaurant was delivered to your table on a conveyor belt or from holes in the roof? What possibilities would open up if you could wash your clothes at home without using water? What if your bed could gently vibrate you awake in the mornings?

Some of those ideas either already exist or are being

tested. Some of them I just made up. The point is that true entrepreneurs seek inspiration from everything they do, everyone they speak to, anything they touch or engage with.

They look around themselves and ask: "What if?"

Read widely and outside of your industry. Flick through *Vanity Fair* and *Accountancy Age*, *Men's Health* and *The Economist*. Look for styles, trends, and influences. Get input from odd sources. Go to a ballet, an amusement park, and then a football match and see how they each deliver customer service. Buy your next meal from a train station and have breakfast on the other side of town. Ask your nephews and nieces about their favorite toys and then the staff at a health club or a retirement home about their frustrations and opinions. Ask your friends about their biggest gripes at work. Take note of what works and special note of the awful experiences you have.

Look back at history for ideas too. What might have been considered unfashionable or kitsch by one generation is often regarded as retro and suddenly fashionable again by the next.

Seek out new experiences. New experiences generate ideas and ideas are the currency of entrepreneurs. What different or eccentric activity are you going to do today?

Transform, transact, or transcend

There are lots of ways for a business to make money, but they boil down into three broad categories:

1. You could transform materials for a living – converting raw materials into finished goods. That might be taking spools of cotton, silk, and wool, and turning them into high-fashion garments. Taking raw ingredients and turning them into elaborate cakes for celebrations. Or even collecting disused computers from waste tips and recycling the parts to sell back to computer manufacturers.

2. You could build a business that transacts with customers for a living – handling straightforward interactions with customers that could be scripted or even automated. That could be processing bank payments on behalf of corporate customers. Fixing a basic number of mechanical problems with cars. Or offering shiatsu massages to stressed parents.

3. You could set up a business that tries to transcend the norm in its interactions with customers – offering a complex service focused on brain power, tricky decision-making, and advice for difficult problems. Seeking ways to invest your customers' money in order to provide for their retirement. Helping families to design their dream living spaces. Recommending ways for corporate customers to reduce their carbon emissions and be seen as more environmentally friendly.

In your career, you have probably focused on one sort of business. But in considering what kind of a business to set up, keep your mind open to new opportunities.

Go 3D

Economists aren't reputed to be the most fun people in the world but they did spot that there's always money to be made from doing what others either can't or won't do – the so-called 3D jobs that are difficult, dirty, or dangerous.

Of course the real money is in the jobs that are all three.

As long as it's legal and you're meeting a customer need, why not do it? It goes without saying that you'll want to wake up in the mornings and do it too. However, remember that you don't need to be doing the difficult, dirty, or dangerous.

I know an entrepreneur who has grown a business out of providing residential cleaners. With his success in the residential market, he is now looking to tackle corporate contracts too. Another entrepreneur has masterminded the acquisition of individual funeral homes and brought them together to form a mini-conglomerate that offers better service at lower cost. I know another outfit that collects, returns, and launders babies' nappies – a service that well-to-do mothers seem happy to pay for in order to salve their environmental consciences.

Of course you may not get excited about the idea of washing a dirty nappy. I can well understand that you may not want to run round other people's homes and clean their toilets for them but then I'm not saying that you need to get passionate about it. Those are service businesses. If you can get excited about the idea of hiring people and providing customers with a service, the type of service itself may not be an issue.

Treasure absolutely any opportunity you come across. Don't disregard the difficult, dirty, or dangerous. What someone else snubs could just be the perfect opportunity for you.

Play 20 questions

Still stuck for those elusive ideas? Looking for that light bulb to flicker on in your head? It's time to play 20 questions:

1. What hobbies do you have?
2. What do you love doing?
3. When were the last five occasions you had fun?
4. What are your three biggest talents?
5. What have you seen abroad that you wish you had at home?
6. Is there something you love that you can't find?
7. What irritates you as a consumer?
8. What service or product would you buy today if it existed?
9. What complaints do your friends have as customers and consumers?
10. What is your favorite shop and how could it be better?
11. What could save you time and money if only you could find it?
12. Who do you think provides great service and how could it be transferred to a new product or service?
13. What would help people to have more fun in their lives?
14. What could you produce faster, better, or cheaper?

15. What would help your colleagues to get out of the office on time?
16. How could you make someone feel safer and happier?
17. What could you do to help a parent save a few minutes every day?
18. Who do you think has an indispensable product but dire service?
19. What do you think people tolerate – but don't need to?
20. What experience would enable people to enjoy their lives more?

Go against the crowd

Successful entrepreneurs often talk about the struggles they had in their early days: about their battles to convince skeptical investors, persuade suppliers, educate customers, and deal with incredulity and apprehension from just about everyone every single step of the way. However, the feeling that you are swimming upstream can be a good thing.

More worrying is when everyone thinks that your idea is a good one. If you have spotted that lots of people seem to be going in a certain direction, be wary not to jump on the bandwagon. Avoid at all costs following them with a me-too strategy, hoping to emulate their success with only a mindless variation on whatever seems popular at the moment.

Just look back on those dot-com wannabes of only a few years ago. Everyone wanted to do something with the internet but how many of them made money out of it? Some of the big players such as Amazon, Yahoo, and eBay have thrived, but the guys and gals trying to mimic their success have disappeared without trace. More recent successes such as social networking site MySpace and video sharing site YouTube have created new interest in what has been dubbed Web 2.0. Can you name any of the entirely forgettable businesses that they spawned, though? Probably not.

Harness the power of three

Being an entrepreneur can be lonely at times, but coming up with an idea need not be. When you play 20 questions, there's no reason to do it alone. Market researchers are always polling consumers on the street, pestering them with phone surveys, and running focus groups with carefully selected ~~victims~~ volunteers – they wouldn't keep doing it if it didn't deliver results. Learn from those cunning market research folks and harness the brainpower of your friends to come up with that breakthrough business idea.

Gather a group of friends for a bit of a brainstorming session. You can run it as formally or informally as you like – do it down the pub, over coffee, perhaps over takeaway on your kitchen table – but remember that these are your friends and they are doing you a favor. To get results, wine and dine your friends and make sure the session is lighthearted and fun. Get unusual combinations of your friends together and repeat as necessary.

The aim is to find an antidote to the sameness and safeness that goes on elsewhere – to throw around ideas that are provocative, unconventional, even odd. Just remember the crucial rule of brainstorming: no one is allowed to criticize any idea, no matter how ridiculous it might at first seem. Each person can only build on the ideas of other people, not destroy them. Encourage the zany and ridiculous because one of them might just lead to the breakout idea you need.

Oh, and make sure you find some way of keeping track of the ideas. Perhaps a tape recorder or even scribbling thoughts on Post-It notes.

Hang on, you might be wondering, why the power of three? I reckon you won't get enough buzz if there are only two of you but feel free to have a few more people if you like. On the other hand, don't go much above six or seven. If you have eight friends who would like to help out, you would be better off running two separate brainstorming sessions to get the most out of them.

It won't be long before you might have the kernel of a workable business concept.

Scribble before you sleep

The land between your waking and sleeping lives is a fertile one for the brain. The brain starts to switch off its conscious, rational thinking processes, and its creative, irrational ones start to kick in.

So have a notepad by your bed.

As you drift off to sleep and your conscious brain cedes control to your unconscious, ideas can sometimes bubble up to the surface. The fragments of dreams that you can remember in the morning might provide a few ideas too.

OK, 90 percent of them may be rubbish ideas. But, hey, one in ten isn't a bad hit rate, is it?

Trust your gut

The right idea will eventually hit you like a bullet to the head. Only with less blood and risk of death, but hopefully just as forcefully.

The first barrier to turning an idea into a business is the one you need to overcome for yourself. If you aren't excited by the idea, you're not going to work long days and long, long months bringing it to fruition. If you aren't convinced by the idea, you won't be able to convince others about it.

I'll keep this one short and to the point.

Trust your instincts, your feelings. If you feel good about it, that's a start. Capture your ideas on paper and leave it until the next day. If you go to bed with the idea and wake up still eager about it, you might be onto a winner.

Think buyer, not seller

You have a passion for skiing and want to open a skiwear boutique but you live in a sunny clime. Do you have a market?

Building a viable enterprise has only one key: it's about providing a product or service that someone will pay for. Even at this early stage of throwing ideas around, try to think about the potential customer for whatever you might do. Which isn't to say that your hypothetical love of skiing has to be quashed. You could align yourself with a travel agent that specializes in winter breaks. You could move to a cold country. You could build a dry ski slope or even import snow machines and create a winter wonderland. However, make sure you are realistic about whether doing any or all of those will send enough paying customers your way.

Too many entrepreneurs produce skillfully crafted products or design incredible services. They offer goods that are exquisite or clever, beautiful or radical. However, they go out of business because they can't connect with enough customers willing to buy them. The dot-com boom was a perfect example of entrepreneurs who found interesting ways to use technology but ultimately failed to solve business problems or tap into genuine needs; much of the web today continues to be interesting and innovative, but full of solutions in search of problems. Just because you can do it doesn't mean that people will want it and want to pay for it.

Don't fall into that same trap.

The most successful entrepreneurs do not merely create something and then try to sell it – they find out what customers need and then create it. Rather than outsmart the customer, they offer something that smart customers need.

If there is a mantra for you to repeat without fail, it is this: have a customer for what you do. Don't assume that customers will be as excited by your idea as you are. Just because your product or service may be good or better or great does not mean that customers will part with money for it. Even throwing lots of money at it through a slick marketing campaign probably won't do it either.

Modern customers do not simply buy what you tell them to buy. Unless what you offer fulfills some want or need of customers, it won't sell. It's a hard fact of business and one you need to learn now.

Ignore the nay-sayers

People will knock your idea – but that's OK – it's human nature to resist new ideas. The newer or more unusual your idea, the less likely people are to see its potential.

Back in 1876, the president of Western Union announced that Alexander Graham Bell's telephone was no more than an "electric toy" and that Bell's idea of putting one in every home was "utterly out of the question."

In 1903, a Michigan banker declared with great certainty that Henry Ford's automobile was a mere novelty and that "the horse is here to stay."

Only ten years ago, if you'd asked someone whether they would be willing to buy secondhand clothes from a total stranger in Albuquerque, they would have laughed at the idea. Of course nowadays over 80 million people do pretty much that on eBay every year.

However, lack of vision is only one reason people might tell you your idea isn't going to work. There are unfortunately people in the world who can't bear to see others succeed. They might feel stuck in their jobs and unable to get out. They probably long to become entrepreneurs but lack the creativity or courage to do so. And they find it easier to pour cold water on the dreams of others than to say anything positive.

Then there are the people who might be genuinely concerned for you. In their eyes, they see you as too naive or inexperienced to run your own business. They worry that you're taking too big a gamble; they feel that you're throwing away the security of income and career.

Know what? People have been shaking their heads and grunting "it'll never work" since our predecessors discovered fire and invented the wheel. As a species we've done pretty well at coming up with still more ideas and innovation, and it's your turn next.

03

Deepening Understanding Around Your Idea

You have a great idea for starting a business now. It's shrewd, it's timely, and it's bubbling away inside you like liquid excitement. But you need to forge it into something more tangible by understanding the reality of your situation.

An idea that is only in your head is of no use to anyone. An idea with no link to reality has no worth, no value. Only when you test your concept against what is happening in the real world can you evaluate whether you can turn it into a business. It's no good having an idea that is "ahead of its time" if it is so far in advance of the market that you can't make money from it. Neither are you going to succeed if someone else is already doing it.

The bottom line is how to make money from your idea. To get the right product at the right price and at the right time for customers to want to buy it. You won't know that until you understand the market – the customers and competitors, the suppliers, trends, and size of the opportunity.

This next phase is about gaining more information and understanding. As you do so, you will gradually turn your fuzzy idea into a clear vision of what you will offer to your customers.

Begin to create your vision

In the months to come, you will need to talk to many, many people about your offering. You will need to educate and explain, instruct and enthuse, tempt and convince all manner of people about what you want to do with your business.

So settle for yourself exactly what it is you plan to offer to your customers. Paint a picture in your head of how it will look and feel. Call it a vision or simply a clear image of what your offering will look, smell, taste, or feel like. Think about its features and benefits, its uniqueness, the type of customer who will buy it, how it will be delivered, and so on. Picture it in as much detail as you can. And if any of the details are unclear, well, that's obviously something you will need to work on.

You may not have all of the answers at first, but you should at least start to think about questions such as:

- What are the key features of your product or service? What makes it distinctive, technically superior, exciting, or even unique?
- How does your offering differ from what is already available or similar?
- Most importantly, what are the key benefits of your

offering? Features describe what it is, but benefits describe what it does and why someone should buy it.

- Under what circumstances do you see your customers buying from you?
- Would you buy your own product? Why?
- Who are your *ideal* customers? Are they women aged over 45 or children between the ages of 6 and 10? Are they small business owners who need to free up some of their time or IT directors with a budget of millions?
- Realistically, who are your *likely* customers? Of course everyone wants educated customers with plenty of money to spend, but is that realistic?
- How do you see customers finding their way to you? Just as examples, will you visit potential customers in person or advertise on the radio, offer one-click shopping on the internet or tempt customers into visiting your showroom, salon, or store?
- Why should customers buy what you have to offer rather than any others that are already available?

No one expects you to be able to have it all mapped out from day one, but it will need working through at some stage. If you can't see it clearly in your own mind, how are you going to explain it to investors and customers?

Understand why customers buy

The customer is king. Long live the king (or queen). However, understand that the king is often an irrational beast. Customers rarely buy purely because an offering is high quality. No matter how educated or experienced the customer, the customer is still only human, and humans make decisions as much for emotional as rational reasons.

Let's take a few examples. Fast-food purveyors McDonald's thrive on selling Happy Meals to parents not because of the quality of the plastic toys, but because the toys allow the parents precious minutes of peace and quiet during meal times. Companies such as Gucci and Louis Vuitton do not merely sell clothing and products; they sell an aura of status, sophistication, and luxury that allows consumers to feel rich, glamorous, successful, and beautiful. Apple iPods sell as much for the grace of their fit and finish as for their functionality.

It's quite straightforward really. Customers buy for one of two reasons. Either a product makes them feel good or it avoids them feeling bad.

On the good side, maybe it makes customers feel calm or secure or satisfied or superior to their friends. Perhaps it helps them feel pampered or loved or safer or at peace with themselves.

Avoiding bad feelings may be to do with reducing the pain, hassle, guilt, or frustration they might otherwise feel. Or the best reason of all is that your product or service saves them money (or the pain of having to spend more money elsewhere).

See? If what you are proposing to offer doesn't do one of the two, you run the risk of developing a solution in search of a problem. Only when you can make your customers feel good about themselves or solve their problems will you find them happily embracing your offering and evangelizing about it.

Keep your forward momentum

I know it's a cliché, but I shall repeat it anyway. Success at being an entrepreneur is 1 percent inspiration, and 99 percent perspiration.

Just because a saying has become a cliché does not mean that it is not true. Lots of people have ideas. In fact I would be surprised if you came up with a genuinely novel idea that no one else in the world has ever considered. But ideas do not turn themselves into businesses.

Lots of people think they could have written *The Da Vinci Code* or the *Harry Potter* books, but only Dan Brown and J. K. Rowling did. Ideas are commonplace. Ideas are not what matters. It's putting in the effort to turn an idea, a notion, or a thought into a commercial reality. So take that next step from merely thinking about your idea.

Seriously though, many would-be entrepreneurs lose faith at this point. They have the idea but procrastinate, managing to convince themselves that they are leaving it until a better time. Perhaps after you get your end-of-year bonus, maybe after you have moved house or after the baby is born.

True entrepreneurs take their ideas and take action straightaway. Savvy entrepreneurs realize that a gap of even a few months could be the difference between being the leader in a new market and merely one of a host of wannabes and never-wills.

If you are still juggling the demands of a full-time job, you probably only have a handful of hours each week to begin researching and testing the market, and turning your idea into a plan. However, even that handful of hours will already take you beyond the 95 percent of the population who may have an idea but take it no further.

Leave it up to the others to dream, wish, or wonder what might have been.

Research the reality

Of course you want to cultivate, cherish and protect your kernel of an idea, but at some point you must unleash your idea on the big, bad world where competitors will be watching and ready to stamp on your venture, and where customers will choose whether to buy what you have to offer.

In negotiating such trials, research will help you to present your offering in the best way possible. Look for ways to understand the competition, suppliers, customers, and market trends.

Start by reading voraciously about your chosen field. Soak up industry knowledge through the trade and professional press, sign up for internet newsletters, and spend hours searching the World Wide Web. Remember though that even in an age in which Google seems to rule the world, a lot of information is still to be found only in old-fashioned books. For periodicals, directories, and reports, you may need to leave your computer and visit a business school, university, or trade association library.

Study your chosen industry and try to answer questions such as:

- What is the total size of the market (i.e. how much do customers in this sector spend in total on offerings similar to yours)?
- What trends have you seen affecting this sector in the past? What trends are likely to dominate in the future? What threats and opportunities do these trends present for you?
- What issues is the industry facing?
- Who are the main players – the competitors – in this field?
- How do your competitors stack up in terms of size, offering, pricing, and so on?
- What are the features and benefits that your competitors are able to offer?
- Who are the main suppliers in this industry? And do they supply what you need?

These are the sorts of questions that investors or banks will want to know should you require funding. And all of this will inform your ability to present your offering to customers in the best way too.

Network as if your life depended on it

Networking. It's a big part of the entrepreneurial game. Especially true in the early stages when you are looking to soak up hints and tips and tricks of the trade, insider gossip, speculation on market trends, and news about the area of business that you have decided to enter.

Desk research can only get you so far. People will always be your biggest resource. People will have access to the latest stories, rumors, and trends that may not make it into any report for a good year or more.

So. Your mission, should you choose to accept it (and you would be stupid not to), is to talk to just about anyone and everyone who might want to spend a few minutes with you. Get ready to smile and ask questions and nod politely and absorb like the proverbial sponge.

Go to forums, trade shows, seminars, conferences, and exhibitions. Often you may learn less from the presenters and keynote speakers than from mingling with the other delegates and soaking up information. Flatter potential competitors and suppliers – subtly, of course – and ask their opinion.

Likewise, go to school reunions, alumni dinners, and parent–teacher committee meetings too. An old school friend might now run a venture capital firm. An ex-colleague's new partner might be a journalist who writes for an industry journal.

Go and listen to suppliers' sales presentations too. Sit through them and ask questions about the economics of the industry – who does what and when and for how much? Even if you are sure you will not buy from a supplier, go and meet with them and ask questions. Challenge them to make their offering viable and relevant to you. You never know. You might just learn something, or you might change your mind and end up working with them anyway.

They say never to mix business with pleasure. Personally, I'd like to know who they are because if you are truly excited about your work, you should want to talk about your work to your friends. Your business should be your pleasure. That way, you won't be so put out about having to give up evenings and weekends in the quest for contacts and information.

Keep attending events until you have had enough. And then go attend some more because networking is a numbers game. You can never predict when you might meet someone who has a useful contact or when someone will let a useful piece of information slip. But, as Americans like to say, "you do the math." If you meet ten times as many people, you're ten times as likely to succeed.

Ask, listen, evaluate

Talk to anyone and everyone even vaguely related to your field. Just because you may be launching a business selling garden furniture doesn't mean that an accountant who has never dealt with garden furniture might not have some insights on the world of business finances. Just because you intend to specialize in publishing women's literature doesn't mean that another entrepreneur can't offer advice on the trials of starting a business.

Listen to what people have to say. Encourage them to be honest rather than polite – you want candor, not diplomacy – but evaluate, assess, and weigh up the value of what they say. Hardly anyone will ever admit that they don't know the answer to a question; everyone has an opinion if you only care to ask for it.

Look out for the liars though. That's right, people who will look you in the eye but knowingly tell you an untruth. A few may lie to protect your feelings. Suppliers and consultants may obscure the truth because they want to sell you their products or charge you for their time. Competitors may try to throw you off course to protect trade secrets and deter a potential rival.

Never accept what people tell you as gospel truth. Look for recurring themes and patterns in what people say rather than taking every single one of them at their word. Use your brain to differentiate the facts from the fiction.

Ask the right questions

It's inevitable that people will shake their heads, say that your concept won't work, and warn you off trying. Quite earnestly, they will tell you it can't be done your way. Or at least they will do unless you ask them the right questions.

Most of the negative people you meet do not intend to be difficult. Whether they are suppliers, customers, competitors, or industry commentators, they may simply lack the perspective to be able to see how your idea could work.

It's your job to help them to help you. Encourage them to think a little harder and open up to the possibility of how it might work.

For example, if people say it's impossible, ask: "What

would need to change to make it possible?" Your question will cause them to furrow their brow, rub their chin, and wonder what conditions might need to be in place for your idea to come to fruition.

If people say it can't or won't work, ask: "What alternatives are there?" Encourage them to think of other shapes that your idea might take.

They might say that something is too difficult. Well, difficult isn't the same as saying it is impossible. So ask: "I realize it's going to be difficult, but what would be the first step to take to making it happen?"

Never take a refusal as your final answer. Use questions to urge and encourage the people you meet to consider options and alternatives. Swiftly, you will find the inconceivable being downgraded to merely improbable or even merely difficult. And if that's not a challenge waiting to be accomplished, what is?

Be discreet

Passion and enthusiasm are qualities that an entrepreneur cannot have enough of. Be generous with your manner; just be prudent with your words. Give out too much detail to the wrong audience and you could shoot your business down before it has had a chance to fly.

True, 99 percent of businesses are not based merely on the inspiration but also the perspiration to turn it into a reality. But when you're networking with other business-people, they might just have the resources and desire to take your ideas and run with them.

You might be wise to talk in general terms rather than going into the details. Laugh and change the subject. Whisper that you can't say exactly what you are doing for now. Explain that all will be revealed in a few months' time. Anything.

On the other hand, never tell an outright lie about your aims. There's a line between discretion and lying that must never be crossed. You will encounter many people with whom you may need to foster long-term relationships. Having them catch you spinning total falsehoods in the early days of your business – even when it is to protect your company's secrets – hardly starts the relationship on the right footing.

Be enthusiastic by all means. But be careful too.

Understand the competition

Doesn't matter how good you are if the competition is better. So, go and unravel exactly what your competitors are offering.

Now, you may say that what you are proposing to offer is unique and has no direct competitors. But everyone has competitors. Even if you are offering a new type of food that is sourced from another planet, your competition is all the sorts of food on Earth that consumers might decide to buy instead. You just need to work out what other businesses are the most likely rivals for your potential customers' time, attention, and (most importantly of all) money.

Visit your competitors and get a grasp of the feel and atmosphere and total experience that they offer. Become a customer and figure out what you do and don't like about their products and services. Walk into their stores or branches, pretend you are a potential customer and get the sales people to run their sales pitches past you. Make a purchase, make a complaint. Feel the quality of the furnishings in their showrooms, listen to the type of music they have playing over the airwaves.

If it's a retail concept you're looking at, keep going back to different stores owned by each competitor to get a sense of what the company is trying to offer as a whole. Spy on other customers and watch the sales staff. Note what the customers buy, how much they spend, how they react to the whole experience.

Visit their websites, drop by their online store and make a purchase. Send off for their brochures or invite one of their sales associates to call you. Sign up for their newsletters and raid their websites for ideas.

What does each of your competitors do well or badly? If something works well, think about how you could replicate it or add your own twist to it. If something works badly, think about how you could do it quicker, safer, friendlier, better.

Research your customers

Find customers who are willing to buy what you produce and you have a business. But the type of customers and how much they are willing to spend will determine whether your business is barely profitable or awash with money.

Customer research takes long hours and patience to find enough customers who are willing to talk. Market research consultancies would of course happily charge you enormous fees to do it for you, but at this early stage of turning your vision into a more concrete proposal, you would be better off doing it for yourself.

Some more questions for you to consider:

- Who are your customers? Do they have common characteristics that can be built into a profile of your "typical" customer?
- What are their buying habits? What, how much, and how often do they buy?
- Why do they buy? Are the reasons customers say they buy the same as the reasons you think they buy? For example, customers prefer to say that they buy designer labels because of quality and never because of prestige, social cachet, or sexiness.
- How much do they pay for what's currently on offer? How much might they be willing to pay for what you could offer?
- What do they like or dislike about the offerings that are presently on offer? And can you fulfill any needs that are currently not being met?

Recognize that the final choice is yours

You may find that gathering customer information is the most difficult piece of research to get right. Not so much because it is difficult to get in front of customers but because of their complex psychology.

Customers are often limited in their imagination by

what is currently on offer. The more different or even radical your offering, the more likely customers are to struggle to understand how it might fit into their world. They might shake their heads about your offering and say they wouldn't buy it when you ask them about it, only for them to love it when you give them the opportunity to experience it for real.

However, it works the other way around too. Customers can over-promise but under-deliver. They don't always know their own minds. Without realizing it, they may tell you what they aspire to as opposed to what they would actually do. Take health as just one example. Of course people say they would like to eat more salads and fewer burgers, smoke less, and exercise more, but when it comes to the crunch, they can't – or won't – change their behavior. Be careful not to get carried away by your potential customers' words. Intention does not always translate into action.

I realize this insight that customers don't always get it right may be less than helpful. You can do all the customer research you like in the world but there are no guarantees. It's entirely conceivable that 90 percent of your potential customers may say that they would buy your product but change their minds once you have put it on a shelf. That's the risk that all entrepreneurs have to take.

Use customer research to inform your thinking. Listen to their thoughts and look for patterns. Take on board their suggestions to shape your proposition. And see how they fit into the grand scheme of everything else you have learned about business and social trends. But understand that customer research will never guide you infallibly to an answer; you must ultimately trust your instinct and judgment to decide what to do.

Document your travels

Buy a sturdy notepad, a digital camera, and a comfortable pair of walking shoes.

Into your notepad should go facts and statistics. You might need them later when you are writing a business plan and convincing investors or bankers to furnish you with money. Take notes on everything you find interesting, useful, or unusual. If you spot a sofa or desk or shelving unit you like, ask the owner of the store or premises where they got it. Just make sure you do it in a nonchalant "pretending to be a customer" rather than an intense "getting you to reveal your trade secrets" kind of way.

Use that digital camera to take photos of everything – a shelf display that you like, the way a luxury goods store displays its luggage next to the leather belts, the way a restaurant sets out its menu. Did you know that some businesses actually hire professional corporate spies to go to investigate their competitors? I don't think you need to go that far. Just take a camera and a colleague and pretend you are taking photos of your colleague. Or use your mobile phone to call your own voicemail and leave lengthy messages describing what you see.

As for the walking shoes. Well, you don't want sore feet, do you?

04

Planning and Funding Your Business

Entrepreneurship arguably consists of two steps. The first is one of *exploration*, of using intuition and observation to identify some means of competitive advantage. The second is one of *exploitation*, of turning an idea into a plan and a business that can be sold for money. And now it's time to exploit what you have so far spent time only exploring.

The time will come to communicate your vision to customers and, unless you are in the happy minority of entrepreneurs who can afford to fund their own venture, you may need to approach banks or investors. Before you can do any of that, though, you need to turn your vision into a plan.

A vision in your head is still pretty much only a dream or a wish. It's easy to get romantic or idealistic about the notion of running your own business, but the reality of running your own business is complex and messy and fraught with tangible issues. You need to work through those issues; you need to ground your vision in reality. It's time to write a business plan.

Get it on paper

Trust me, you need a business plan. Even if you think you are setting up an incredibly straightforward business or have decided to offer your services as a freelancer, it's worth writing a plan. Even if you think you have it all worked out in your head, you might be surprised it doesn't quite come out as coherently when you need to explain it to a customer. A business plan helps you to crystallize your ideas, clarify your goals, and prepare to explain it to other people. It encourages you to focus on exactly what you need to do and pushes you to think about the practicalities of founding your venture.

Writing a business plan is as much about clarifying your goals for yourself as it is to communicate your goals and persuade others. If you can't write a plan that makes sense to yourself, how will you explain it to investors, suppliers, and customers?

In fact, a business plan sounds more formal than it actually is. You don't need an MBA to write one. If you have ever planned a party or arranged a family holiday or budgeted a project at work, you can write a business plan. A business plan is merely a set of steps outlining what you are going to do and when you are going to do it. If your business is a destination, then a business plan is the road map that will take you from wanting to get there to being there. Writing it all out helps to make your ideas concrete and clarifies your goals.

How much money do you need to get the business off the ground? When will you start making money? How much money will you make and when will you earn enough to cover your costs? What kind of staff might you need to hire? Where will you get those staff from?

A business plan forces you to think about the major issues that all successful businesses have to contend with. A lot of entrepreneurs avoid writing business plans. A lot of businesses fail. Think there might be a link?

Use a plan template

Temptation is a terrible thing. If you don't like the idea of writing a business plan, you might be tempted to pay an accountant, marketing consultant, or other expert to produce one for you. However, I think that's a big mistake. Huge.

An expert will happily take your fee and write a plan for you, but if your business fails, they're not going to get too distraught about it. Do you think it will ruin their lives? No, of course not. But it could ruin yours.

You are the person who needs to calculate exactly how the business will make money. You are the person who needs to understand how to keep a steady stream of customers coming back to buy from you again and again and again. If you need to seek funding, you are the person who will have to pitch the business plan to banks or investors. You are the person who will need to explain it to potential employees, not your accountant, marketing consultant, or expert.

But have no fear. There are plenty of resources showing you how to write a business plan. Go online and type the words "business plan template" into Google or your favorite search engine and in a fraction of a second you will be inundated by dozens of templates.

You'll notice that business plan templates can vary – sometimes quite significantly – but then you wouldn't expect the business plan for a manufacturing business to have the same detail in it as one for a service company. Choose the headings that suit you. Decide what information you need for your own business. I don't want to force-feed you a definitive set of business plan headings, because there isn't one. If, for example, you are approaching different banks, they may ask you to use their particular templates.

However, key headings should probably include:

- Overview of the business – what does your business do?
- Products and services – what are the advantages and disadvantages, features and benefits of what you plan to offer? How much will you sell them for?
- The market – who are the customers? Who are the competitors? What is the size of the market and the size of the opportunity?
- Marketing plan – how will you promote your product and get customers to notice your business and offering?
- Operational plan – what practical steps must you take to get your business up and running and selling to customers?
- Financial plan – how much money will you need to start up the business? How much money do you expect to make every week or month for the first year of your business?

- Credentials of the management team – who are the people that will steer the business and make it happen? What skills and experience do you/they have that will make the business a success?

KISS the numbers

Spreadsheets and financial forecasts – don't you just love 'em? No? The good news is that you don't have to.

A good business plan will include a profit and loss account, projections and forecasts. But you can get someone else to work those up for you. All you need to do is understand the overall financial strategy for the business. That can be summed up in five words: "sales minus costs equals profit."

You may have heard entrepreneurs talking about doing their numbers on the back of a cigarette packet, a beer mat, an envelope. And it really is that easy.

KISS your numbers. Keep It Short and Simple. Because it makes very good sense to start your financial calculations on a single sheet of paper rather than a spreadsheet. If you can estimate these key numbers in the simplest form possible, you can explain them to anyone. You can understand the reality of your costs and how much you will have to sell in order to make money.

Take a blank sheet of paper and write the next 12 months of the year along the top of the page. If you are reading this in June, start with July. Write "sales," "costs," and "profits" along the side. Then write the figures under each month to determine your overall profit forecast for your first year.

If you are going to sell cashmere jumpers for 120

Pounds, Dollars or Yen each, how many are you likely to sell each month? Will you sell the same number in midwinter as the summer? If you are selling consultancy days to clients, will you sell as many during holiday months as the rest of the year?

Don't worry about the minor digits. Think in terms of thousands (or hundreds). And don't forget to take into account that it may take several months to get the business running, in which you will incur costs but probably little or no sales.

Very simple. Very straightforward.

Take a look at the numbers; grimace at them and ponder

Table 1

	Jan	Feb	Mar	Apr	May	Jun	Jul	Aug	Sep	Oct	Nov	Dec
Sales	0	0	0	4	6	7	4	4	7	8	9	10
Costs	6	6	3	3	3	3	3	3	3	3	3	3
Profit	-6	-6	-3	1	3	4	1	1	4	5	6	7

Total first year profit assuming no sales for the first three months = 17.

---

a bit more; maybe shake your head in disbelief. Then put them aside. Go away and come back to them later. Review the assumptions you have made regarding your sales and costs. Will you really be able to generate those sales figures in so few months? How sure are you of the investment it will take in your early months?

Eventually, you will crack the question of how much profit you might make in your first year. Congratulations – you have the first draft of your financial plan.

Put your money where your passion is

Let's talk about money again. The rule for making money from your outfit is very simple. The more you put in, the more you can later take out. And the more someone else puts in, the less you can later take out.

Told you it was simple.

Banks and investors do not provide entrepreneurs with money out of the goodness of their hearts. They want a return, and until they get that return, they will monitor your efforts, push you in directions you may not want to go, and do whatever they can to ensure they get that return.

If you can possibly go it alone without outside money, then do it. Reduce your outgoings, raid your savings, and put your money where your passion is.

Entrepreneurs who are setting up their own consultancies or working as freelancers are the most likely to be able to afford to go it alone because the costs of setting up a home office or even renting premises won't be that high. However, if you are in a technology business or have a physical product that needs prototyping and manufacturing, or you need to invest in a large physical space such as a boutique or restaurant, you may have no choice but to approach banks and investors.

Putting your own money into your venture is not just about maximizing your return. It's about financial discipline too. Trust me when I say you will be so much more careful with your own money than when it is someone else's. You might be tempted to buy new laptops for yourself and the rest of the team. You might like the idea of working with a famous architect or an award-winning designer. Perhaps you have seen some nifty-looking office furniture that oozes class and sophistication. But do you really need them? Entrepreneurs spending other people's money will tend to say yes. Entrepreneurs spending their own money are far more likely to say no, saving them precious cash, and ensuring they have enough money to spend on the important stuff to get their businesses launched.

You get the picture. Now do what you must.

Take the plunge

A lot of entrepreneurs start off working on their new ventures in their spare time while juggling day jobs. Which is fine in the early days. But once you have researched your idea and made a plan, you should let nothing stop you from committing entirely to your new career.

Entrepreneurship is hard enough work without having to sink a large portion of your energies into working for someone else too. You need to take the plunge and quit your existence as a wage slave. Quit so that your new venture can become the sole focus for your energies and passion rather than merely the hobby you tinker with when you aren't doing your "proper" job. Otherwise you will always be able to retreat to the safety of your day job, its familiarity, and the steady income.

Bear in mind that your potential customers' tastes are constantly changing and your competitors are always on the lookout for new ideas. If you procrastinate and don't act quickly enough on your business idea, someone else surely will.

Develop your elevator pitch

Ping. You step into an elevator (or lift, depending which side of the Atlantic you're on) and there's your favorite and very rich entrepreneur. You have 15 seconds to pitch your business before he or she gets out on the tenth floor. What do you say?

Call it an elevator pitch, a spoken logo, a blurb, or a spiel. Whatever you call it, it's the stuff of business lore. Whether you are looking to entrance an investor or grab the attention of a customer, you must think about how you convey your message.

Encapsulate your thoughts in a sharp set of sentences that will beguile your audience and have them asking you for more. But this is no mere advertising slogan. It has to have content as well as charm.

A good elevator pitch should be like a swift one-two punch in a boxing ring. One, hit them in the face (not literally – I don't want anyone writing in saying that they are being prosecuted for actual bodily harm) with the big idea, your premise, your concept. Two, knock 'em to the ground with the biggest benefit, the most compelling and evocative reason why everyone should have one of whatever you are offering.

Short and sweet. Simple and memorable. Because elevators only take 10–20 seconds to get to the right floor before your quarry has escaped. Speak for a minute and you have lost them. Even if they are too polite to have moved on, you have probably still lost their attention.

But don't think you can get away with speaking more quickly to pack more words into those precious seconds either. I don't quote other people much, but I thought this one was perfect. British actor and Hollywood star Sir Michael Caine once observed rather brilliantly in an interview: "The basic rule of human nature is that powerful people speak slowly and subservient people quickly – because if they don't speak fast nobody will listen to them."

Get it right and you could create a verbal banner that you can pass on to your contacts and customers to wave on your behalf too.

So. Think of a sexy way to stand out rather than a mundane way to communicate facts. Write down what you think you may want to say. Read it out loud and listen to your own words. Select more gripping phrases, choose better-sounding words. But remember to consider your pace, pauses, and tone too. Practice it over and over and over until you can say it automatically, charismatically, warmly, enthusiastically.

Seek a mentor

Setting up your own business is the best business education that you can ever get. But surely it wouldn't hurt to have a bit of advice from someone who has been through it all, right?

Mentors who have already achieved some success in business can share their knowledge and insights. They can point out traps and pitfalls to avoid; they can spot short cuts to take. And, if they like you and trust you enough, they might just share their black book of contacts too.

Don't know any successful entrepreneurs? Not a problem. A bit of research and networking will help you find your way to one.

Now, you might wonder why an experienced and successful stranger would want to mentor you. But the truth is that most people are genuinely flattered when they are asked for their advice and opinions. When you start asking around, you will probably find that the biggest barrier is your own reluctance to ask for help rather than other people's lack of interest in wanting to help. You will find that most entrepreneurs are only too happy to at least consider mentoring you – so long as they like you and rate your business idea.

So get out there and start searching. Read your trade press and learn the names of the business-people who have made it in your industry. Look at businesses you admire in your own industry or, failing that, adjacent industries. Depending on the level of ambition you have for your business and the size of the opportunity, look for people who are perhaps 5, 10, or even 15 years ahead of you in the entrepreneurial game.

Next comes a bit of networking and sweet-talking. Senior people usually surround themselves with gatekeepers such as personal assistants to filter out trivial matters and unimportant people (i.e. people like you). But senior people can still be receptive to calls from people they know. So see if your contacts can refer you on to contacts who work within their companies, and see if the contacts of your contacts can refer you to further contacts who might know your would-be mentor well enough to further an introduction. No one said it would be a case of a single phone call to find your ideal mentor, but it is possible.

Eventually you will find yourself in a position to speak with a potential mentor. It may not be with your first-choice mentor or your second, but with persistence you will find your way to one. Just make sure you have your elevator pitch polished and ready.

Treat your mentor as a special resource

Two factors will determine whether a senior figure might be swayed into becoming your mentor. One, he or she must see you as possessing a legitimately credible business idea. So unless you have researched it well and considered the likely size of the opportunity in a plausible business plan, you should expect to get turned down. Two, he or she must want to spend time with you. And here it's about being genuinely passionate. Why wouldn't this person want to work with someone who has a great idea and the passion to transform it into a thriving business?

Ask your mentor about major problems you face and listen to his or her advice and insights. Ask for permission to use your mentor's name when networking with other people as an endorsement of you to open doors that may otherwise remain closed. And, once your mentor trusts you, ask whether your mentor might be able to introduce you to others who might be interested in investing or buying or offering you further advice.

But avoid running to your mentor with every issue or difficulty that you face. Yes, he or she will enjoy working with you and want you to succeed. But your mentor has his or her own businesses to run too. And your mentor will quickly tire of you if you appear to need help with every trivial problem that you encounter. If a very busy, very influential mentor can only see you once a quarter, then respect those wishes. You could always find other mentors to provide advice on a more regular basis. If a mentor can only manage to share a fruit juice with you after a Friday-evening spin class, then that's when you will make yourself available.

Prepare fastidiously before discussions with your mentor. Think of the key questions you want to ask. Put your thoughts in order, have facts and figures ready, and be equipped to deliver a progress report if you are asked to. If you have not prepared and your mentor thinks you are wasting his or her time, you may as well say goodbye to the relationship.

Think of your mentor as a very, very special resource, because he or she is. Finding one is not easy, but having one will pay dividends.

Entice investors with your plan

So you've decided that you really cannot afford to fund your business yourself. Even perhaps by billing customers upfront for a chunk or all of the payment for what you propose to do (it's sneaky, but sometimes works). Seeking external funding requires a hard-sell approach – persuading others that the opportunity to be had from your business is greater than the risks. And they will dwell on the risks, especially if you have no track record of starting up and running businesses.

A loan is always preferable to investment from an external source. Although a bank may require you to jump through many hoops before lending you the money, after that they won't interfere much. The same cannot be said of investors.

If you have enormous start-up costs but the opportunity to make tens if not hundreds of millions, venture capital or private equity firms might be interested. If the sums are much smaller, you might need to target so-called angel investors – rich individuals – who might still be willing to buy into the action. Desk research and shaking hands with lots of contacts will point you in the direction of the right investors to approach for your market.

Whoever you eventually meet, think of presenting your business plan as an extended elevator pitch. Sure, you start with the one-two combination of your big idea and its biggest benefit. But then you need to back it up with the detail, answer all of their questions, handle their objections, and leave them thinking that yours is a business that cannot do anything but succeed.

Build a prototype, create a demo

As a species, we have five senses. We can see and hear, taste, smell, and touch. And the more of those senses you can engage, the easier it will be for you to sell your idea to investors.

A business plan is only words on paper. Even your enthusiasm can only do so much to sell what are otherwise merely words coming out of your mouth. So devise a way for potential customers and investors to engage with what you plan to offer. Think of ways to demonstrate and allow people to test-drive your product or interact with what you plan to sell:

- Build a physical prototype.
- Mock up an artist's rendering or architectural plans.
- Use screenshots and blueprints to help people visualize what you plan to do.
- Bring along a swath of cloth for people to stroke or a gadget with working buttons to push.
- Get samples of your miracle new product for people to touch or taste or smell.

Developing a prototype is often an iterative process. Begin by showing your prototype to a dozen potential customers. Get their feedback and go back to the drawing board. Tweak it and show it to some more customers. Keep tweaking it until you get smiles and nods of agreement from those customers.

Only then should you go to potential investors. Only

when you are able to talk about the modifications you have made and the reactions you get from customers will investors take you seriously.

Interview investors

Maybe I'm being harsh, but I sometimes tell entrepreneurs that accepting money from an investor is like taking cookies from an old lady in a fairy tale. The old lady could merely be a kindly spinster who wants to look after you and see you home safely. Or she could really be an evil witch, with designs on drugging you and sucking the marrow from your bones. Are you ready to have the financial marrow sucked from the bones of your business?

It's fantastic when an investor shows their faith in you by offering to give you a chunk of cash for your business. But you must always consider two questions. First, are you getting the money on the best terms? Consult professional advisers and get the shrewdest, toughest negotiator you can afford to hammer out the very best deal for you.

Second, and more importantly, are these investors the right people to be getting on board? Not all investors are created equally and they should bring more to the deal than merely money. You should expect them to bring information and advice, contacts in the industry, and even management talent with them.

When you are trying to attract their attention, you have to do all the hard work. It is up to you to convince them that you are worthy of their consideration, but when an investor shows serious interest in you, the balance of power tips slowly in your favor. You can talk less and ask more. You should interview them as rigorously as they scrutinize you. Ask them about their track record of working with similar businesses and invite them to remark on possible problems and opportunities that you may not have spotted. Give them the chance to prove that they can help you to succeed more than any other investors.

If investors are buying equity in your business, they will have a considerable say in how your business will be run. A venture capital firm will almost certainly demand a position on your management board and so you had better be happy with what they might have to say. Look for ideas that will add to and improve on your concept. Make sure they complement your vision rather than leading you on a path that might feel uncomfortable to you.

You will be spending a lot of time working together, so remember that their management style and ways of working may be as important as their experience and expertise. Look for an investor who will push you, but not push you over the edge.

Avoid money from family and friends

Banks and investors can be hard taskmasters and so you may be tempted to take a loan from your family or friends instead. If you do that there are no hoops to have to jump through, no complicated paperwork or monthly cash-flow forecasts to have to complete, and these people obviously trust you. However, I would urge you to resist taking this money if you can for three reasons:

1. Family and friends may mean well, but how much do they really know about your business? Unless you can see them being able to contribute directly relevant skills or industry-relevant advice and contacts, walk away. Investment or loan money should come with advice as well as the cash itself.

2. It's like getting an advance on your pocket money when you were a kid. Chances are, you probably didn't end up giving it all back. Money that comes so easily is often just as easily lost. If your business idea really is robust enough, you should be able to convince some bank or investor (although you may have to search harder to do so) willing to share the risk and opportunity with you.

3. What if your venture were to fail? Lose the money and you may end up souring those relationships. Are you prepared to risk the terminal embarrassment plus having those family members or friends shun you for the rest of your life?

Stay positive

Listen to successful entrepreneurs speak about their experiences and you will hear them talk about how they had to persevere. About how they were rejected, snubbed, and refused, and how they were close to giving up – but didn't.

In life there are few guarantees, but I can promise you will suffer knock-backs. You will get rejected from many, many banks. You may meet investors who at first seem interested but then change their minds or, more likely, most just won't be interested at all.

I know that sounds harsh and I don't mean to be disheartening, but it pays to be prepared. To understand that, when you get knocked back for the 43rd time, you need to be able to get back up and get out there, pitching your idea to yet another banker, investor, or customer.

The most formidable barrier to becoming a successful entrepreneur is not to do with investors or banks, suppliers or competitors. It is to do with yourself. There will always be critics to warn you off and tell you that what you are doing is impossible or stupid, can't work or won't work, but you can decide to carry on anyway.

It takes dogged determination to become a successful entrepreneur. But therein lies the good news too, because determination is a quality that is completely within your own control. You don't need an expensive education to get it. You can't buy it. You only need tell yourself at the start of each day that you are choosing to carry on.

It takes guts, willpower, single-mindedness, and persistence. But then, if it were easy, wouldn't everyone be doing it?

Ponder before partnering

Run the business as the sole boss or split the business with partners, the choice is yours. With partners and hopefully a larger combined pool of wealth, you may need to rely less on – or even forgo entirely – the need to approach banks or investors. Partners run the same risks and understand the pressures of running a business and so can also offer comradeship in ways that even great employees simply cannot.

It's tempting to partner with friends, but that can be a dangerous route. Your friendship will certainly be tested and possibly ruined. Look instead for partners who have essential skills, good contacts, and a willingness to work hard to bring your idea to market.

Partners absolutely must have identical aims. Which probably sounds like an obvious statement – you want the business to succeed. But what are your different definitions of success?

I once worked with a group of partners who were all experts in their fields. Unfortunately, their goals were very different. One of the younger partners wanted to grow the business aggressively in the hopes of an eventual trade sale. One of the much older partners was content with the size of the business so long as it provided him with a steady income. Yet another partner had no interest in the financial health of the business and was happy so long as he could pursue the types of project that he personally enjoyed doing. As you might imagine, the business was faltering and fragmented, pulled in multiple directions but going nowhere.

Have a frank discussion with prospective partners and make sure that you not only have identical goals and aspirations, but also have similar working styles and are equally committed to the full-on work that will be needed in making the business a success.

Become equal partners

If you come to the agreement that you need partners, make sure that you all have at least roughly equal influence. Holding on to a 70 percent stake and letting two business partners have 15 percent each is not a partnership – it's giving two employees a feeling of involvement in the business. The business relationship between you would always be unbalanced; it effectively neuters your partners' ability to stand up to you and have a genuine influence in setting the direction of the business.

I've seen too many businesses in which an ego-driven majority owner stamps his or her feet and vetoes great ideas, effectively saying "we're going to do it this way because it's my business." Not because he or she has rational arguments to do it otherwise, but simply because he or she is the biggest shareholder. "It's my party and I'll cry if I want to," anyone?

Shrewd entrepreneurs realize it's better to share the equity and have a smaller stake in a successful business with real growth prospects than remain the majority owner of a tiny business that simply can't grow.

Take heed.

Think the unthinkable

Are you a pessimist or an optimist? Actually, don't answer that because it's a trick question. Entrepreneurs need to be both at the same time. You need the pessimist to consider things that could wrong, but then the optimist has to get on with the job of starting up your business in spite of what could go wrong.

Think of it this way. You would need to take out buildings insurance in case your premises burn down. Doesn't mean you should worry nonstop about it. And it certainly doesn't mean that it should stop you from leasing the premises in the first place.

You should set aside enough time to anticipate possible problems and issues that could derail your business. When figuring out sales and costs, a lot of novice entrepreneurs make overly optimistic projections and don't take into account some of the problems that could arise.

Don't let the problems stop you from starting up. Make contingency plans. Give them enough thought to make your business bulletproof, but don't worry about them so much that you can't think of anything else.

What are the top half-dozen risks for your business? Possible issues could include:

- a competitor opening a similar store in the same street.
- inclement weather – e.g. a mild winter or a wet summer.
- economic recession.
- suppliers putting up the price of raw material or goods – whether it's oil or gas, orchids or silk, oysters or agency staff.
- exchange rate fluctuations.
- the loss of a key member of staff, perhaps through injury or a better job offer.

This isn't about thinking negatively and plunging into a

black pit of despair, but planning sensibly and having a backup plan if things should unfortunately go awry.

05

Setting Up the Business

Next comes the time to work your magic – to lift the words from your business plan and turn them into a trading business with premises, actual employees, real technology, and finally a product or service that your customers can buy.

Entrepreneurs often speak most fondly of this phase. It's the biggest buzz in the world to hold your finished product in your hands or to know that your service is ready to be launched upon the world. So enjoy it and remember that getting to this stage is purely down to your own skill and audacity.

Name your venture

Naming your business is akin to naming a baby. You will probably want to invest special thought into crafting the right name for it and you will want the name to convey a message and herald its uniqueness to the world. However, there are traps to beware of.

The worst trap of all is to name the business after yourself or any business partners such as Peter Donaldson or Jenny Chung or Johnson, Jenkins and West. Any of those businesses could equally be lawyers or plumbers or clothes designers. Unless you are famous in your field and the mere mention of your name automatically gets heads nodding with recognition, don't do it.

Apart from being memorable and easy to pronounce, your company name should tell people what you do and send a message to your relevant customer group. No point calling your business Hazardous Holidays if you are chasing elderly holidaymakers. It's all very well calling a Greek imports company Clytemnestra, but just imagine having to spell it over the telephone time and time and time again.

I chose the name Talentspace for my company because most of what we consult on is to do with identifying and developing talented people. The food chain Pret A Manger is French for "ready to eat," which not only tells the customer that their business is about food, but also implies a certain sophistication by using a French rather than English phrase. The Boston Consulting Group tells the customer squarely that it is a firm of consultants – and an American one at that. And as for The Bathroom Company – well, you would have to be fairly stupid to think it was a firm of accountants.

Invite players to your party

No one is perfect. No one can be good at everything. You have particular weaknesses and blind spots as well as unique strengths and talents. And if you have ever had an appraisal, you will probably have been praised by your boss for your strengths but encouraged to work on your weaknesses.

When you were a wage slave working for someone else, you had no choice but to do what you were told. But you are now an entrepreneur. You are now the boss. So forget about those days and say goodbye to having to work on your weaknesses ever again.

Smart entrepreneurs know that working on their weaknesses can be a big waste of time. Your weaknesses are weak for a reason. You aren't very good in those areas; you probably don't enjoy spending time working on them. So don't spend time on them.

Instead, surround yourself with people who are strong in areas in which you are weak. Avoid at all costs working solely with people just like yourself. No one is perfect, but the right team might just be. If you are not good with numbers, make sure you hire or sub-contract someone who is. If you enjoy setting strategy and thinking about the big picture, enlist someone to work with you who has good attention to detail and can handle the operational stuff. If you like selling gadgets but not making them, find people who will deliver on what you have promised your customers.

Accept your weaknesses for what they are. Just make sure you can recognize them and find others who can pick up the slack.

Get professional advice

You will need professional advice. No matter how determined you are, you simply shouldn't do it all. Sure, you could spend dozens of hours reading up on company law and tax in order to register your company, but is it a good use of your time? You could learn HTML code and the intricacies of a web development package, but unless that is the core concept of your business, wouldn't it make more sense to get someone who knows what they are doing to construct your website for you?

You may need architects, accountants, shop fitters, lawyers, consultants, designers, whatever. The list is almost endless. There can be a bewildering amount of choice out there, so rather than having to decide based on marketing hype, ask your contacts for referrals to good advisers. Then go and meet them. Go to their offices and decide whether you like them, trust them, feel they could do a good job for you. Look at their offices and decide whether they are the kind of advisers who look after people like you. If you are much smaller or larger than their typical client, either could pose problems for you.

Always make sure you meet at least three different firms of each type of adviser you are looking to hire. Part of the reason is to shop around and look for a good price. Once you have fathomed out your prospective advisers, you will be better equipped to decide who can provide you with exactly the right level of support and at just the right price. Never be afraid to haggle. Advisers are used to cutting business deals. Ask for a discount, for a better level of service for the same price, and for deferred payment terms.

But there is another reason to meet at least three sets of advisers. Each adviser you meet will tell you what they can offer you and suggest what they think you need to do.

And you will learn from them. Each adviser will impart some nuggets of information that you probably would not have learned elsewhere. Their sales pitches will inform and educate you, advance your ideas, and suggest directions that you might not at first have considered.

Refine your offering

Beta testing is an indispensable phase of refinement in the world of software and online services. But whatever you do, make sure to fine-tune your product or service until you have created something useful, saleable, desirable.

Everyone loves something for nothing. Look for volunteers to try your product or service and comment on what works and what doesn't. Get them to help you iron out major problems and suggest tweaks. And do it quickly. Product development has traditionally been a fairly tortuous affair of taking a prototype or trial service out to volunteers and getting feedback, analyzing the feedback and deciding what changes to incorporate back into the product or service. And then doing it again and again and again.

Smart businesses realize they cannot afford to spend too long getting their offering right. That wasting too much time could allow a competitor to launch something distressingly similar.

Just make sure you actually listen to your customers. Keep an open mind and be prepared to change your plans. Some entrepreneurs get so wedded to their concept that they see it as an insult when customers report back with negative feedback. It doesn't matter how much trouble you have gone to. It doesn't matter how technically superior your gadget is. It doesn't matter how authentic the ingredients in your secret recipe. Your unabashed goal is to create a product or service that customers will buy.

Never fall into the trap of telling yourself that your customer "doesn't get it." It's your job to refine your product or sharpen your service until they do "get it."

Build the customer experience

What do customers really want when they walk into a café and ask for a cappuccino? Silly question, you might think. Of course they want a cappuccino. But just as importantly, they also want to feel good about themselves. They want to be treated as human beings rather than customers. Indulge a customer's human needs and they will return.

Think about yourself as a customer for a moment. We want the waitress to call us by name and show us to the table that we liked by the window. We want the bookstore owner to remember that we enjoyed a particular book and to recommend another author in a similar vein. The sales associate who backs off when he realizes his product isn't right for you – that kind of behavior garners respect.

Whatever the nature of your business, you will succeed if you can create that same feeling for your customers. Because it's a truth that people do business with people they like.

So here's possibly the only rule to remember: focus on the relationship with your customer. That's right, even more than the tasks you do for them or the products you provide for them.

Customers do not always shop around for the lowest prices. A smile can buy more loyalty than a discount. A genuinely contrite apology for an overcooked steak may win more customer loyalty than a perfect steak in the first place. Customers are rarely entirely rational. They are always looking for ways to connect on a human level with other people. Showing real empathy with the needs and desires of your customers can go a long way.

Corporate buyers look for people they trust more than the lowest price. Because when you are selling, you are effectively making a promise; and corporate buyers know that promises are too often broken. The more complex the project, the more they will look for people who can turn words and promises into actions and results. Establish that trust and you will have them signing big fat checks your way.

Even if yours is a high-tech business, consider how you can use clever sales people, good training, and process design to recreate that personal experience for your customers. It isn't easy if you're in a high-tech, low-touch business, but it's not impossible either.

Clever entrepreneurs focus on the customer experience, ensuring that it is not only reliable and efficient, but warm and friendly, fun and enjoyable too. Manage that and your customers will embrace your business and make it a success.

Map it out from cradle to grave
Products are birthed, orders are placed, customers are fulfilled. Or, hopefully, that's the way it should happen.

To make sure that you can deliver your product or service to customers on time and without fail, it makes good sense to chart all the steps involved. Think about every step of the process from getting in any raw materials you may need to leaving your customers with smiles on their faces.

Of course the precise steps to focus on depend on the nature of your business. A retailer or a baker will have very many more issues around stock and supplies than, for example, a nursery school or a firm of corporate party planners. However, in broad terms, every entrepreneur should consider how the following questions might be relevant:

- How much stock do you need?
- How quickly can you re-order stock? And what alternative arrangements do you have if your preferred supplier has run out?
- Where will you store the stock? Is it safe, secure, insured?
- Who will make the product or provide the service? And what happens if they (or you) are ill, on holiday, or otherwise unavailable?
- Who has responsibility for mundane (but crucial) tasks such as opening up the shop or office every morning, locking it up at night, cleaning your premises, taking bags of cash to the bank, being the first point of contact for incoming calls, and so on?
- How will you handle possible transport or travel arrangements – either for your product or yourself?

- What terms and conditions will you offer around refunds or repairs if customers are not happy?

A service is of little use if it is late. A product that looks good on paper or in the shop is of little use if it arrives in a shoddy condition. Business is about promising you can deliver. And mapping out your business means you will never have to break your promises whenever a customer walks through the door, rings your hotline, or clicks on your website.

Scrutinize your spending

Cash is the lifeblood of the fledgling enterprise. Run out of cash and it's game over. Without it you can't buy raw materials or pay your employees' wages. Oh, and the electric company will probably turn your lights off too.

More businesses collapse because they run out of cash than because they are unprofitable on paper. Now I'm not going to get all technical on you – about how to use sophisticated billing and factoring techniques to manage your cash flow. But being able to minimize your overheads is a critical part of the entrepreneurial mindset.

Only foolish entrepreneurs spend money just because they have it. The clever ones pause, question, and whip out the checkbook only when absolutely necessary. They hire employees only when they are so overloaded by work that they cannot possibly do it themselves – and even then it might be on a part-time rather than full-time basis. They buy good-enough computers with basic configurations to work from, rather than top-of-the-range and state-of-the-art. They buy secondhand office furniture at a third the cost of new. They work from their spare bedroom, a kitchen table, a converted garage. They hold meetings with colleagues at the nearest coffee shop with wireless internet access. They get quotes from three different suppliers every time they want to spend a significant sum of money.

Be frugal and only spend what you must.

In particular it always astounds me when entrepreneurs secure funding and immediately splash it on lavish premises. Now, you might feel that a swanky office will help you win over customers. But in truth most customers are putting their trust in you rather than buying the false aura of wealth that a plush office creates. If anything, customers are more likely to wonder whether they are being ripped off if your offices look too luxurious. The same goes for employees too. They should be excited by the business opportunity – your business premise rather than the premises; they should understand the dirty, hands-on and low-down nature of starting a business. All you need is enough space to cram a few desks in and connections with the outside world through a couple of phone lines.

Bear in mind the principle of return on investment (ROI). Ask yourself: "What is the return on this investment?" Basically, will spending money on something or someone help you to make more money? If hiring a bookkeeper will free you up to do more selling, that's a good ROI. But would, for example, buying classy furniture for your reception area genuinely help your business to make more money than a cheaper set? Probably not.

Work from basic premises, travel economy class and use public transport, shop around and haggle, calculate ROI before spending any money. One day you will be thankful you did.

Get your hands dirty

Starting up is dirty business. Very dirty, in fact. Being an entrepreneur isn't just about coming up with a clever strategy and inveigling investors. It's just as much about implementing it – turning your idea and money into an actual product or service that customers can see and feel or even taste and smell and then buy.

With a watchful eye on cash flow, entrepreneurs end up doing it all themselves. Moving into new premises, you will need to assemble the office furniture, connect your printer to your computer, type your own documents. Fitting out a store or perhaps a restaurant, you will need to roll your sleeves up. Stack the shelves, sweep the floor, unblock the toilet.

Dignified, it's not.

Don't think that entrepreneurship is just the bit where you get to strut around and do the important, strategic stuff. Early entrepreneurship is about doing whatever it takes, whatever is necessary. It's about being practical, not proud.

Immerse yourself in the business

As an entrepreneur, you are the only person responsible for turning your idea and vision into a successful business.

Sure, you may have found wonderful suppliers, lawyers, designers, accountants, architects, surveyors, recruitment consultants, advertising experts, and so on. They may be genuinely excited to be working with you, but their primary concerns are always going to be about the success of their own businesses, not yours.

The reality of being a new business is that you will be just one of many customers to all of these people and they probably have bigger and more important customers too. You will need to fight hard to ensure they all deliver what they do to the quality you require. Put too much trust in them and they will probably let you down. If they have too much to do, which do you think they will prioritize – a new customer like you or one of their key accounts?

Think about it.

If an importer has shipped the wrong consignment to you, you are the one who will have to grovel to your customers, not them. If a web designer misspells the front page of your website, you are the one who looks foolish, not them. If an advertising agency misses a magazine deadline, that could be a month of delays for your business, not theirs. If your business goes belly up, your suppliers get to carry on regardless.

Only you are responsible for your own business.

In much the same way as writing a business plan is a key task for any entrepreneur, you must get involved with everything that goes on when it comes to implementing what you have planned. Make it your focus to oversee everything to the point of being perhaps a little obsessive about it.

Don't let yourself become complacent or assume that your suppliers know what they are doing and are handling it. Yes you need to have an awareness of the big picture in terms of the strategy for your business, but you do need to sweat the small stuff too.

Keep your focus

If you're anything like most entrepreneurs, your mind will be constantly spinning with possibilities. You will notice new opportunities and discover any number of ideas that could be turned into moneymaking products and services for your company.

Be careful not to get diverted off track though. Yes, of course large businesses diversify successfully all of the time. But they possess established, core offerings and have the resources to spare to investigate new ones. You do not – at least not yet.

Keep the original vision for your business in mind. Remind yourself of all the effort you spent researching the market, the customers, suppliers, and competition. Think of the time you have invested in writing a business plan and detailing the steps you needed to take to bring your offering to market. Keep sight of what made your original idea special.

That's not to say you should stay on course regardless. You may need to flex your vision and goals in the light of market developments. Neither should you ignore all new opportunities. Merely wait until your core idea has been turned into a product or service that customers are paying for. Only when your original idea is profitable can you afford to move on to a new idea. Otherwise, you could get distracted – perhaps fatally.

Work smart, not hard

Stop. Hold it right there. Before you start work every day, make sure you engage your brain. Since you don't want to be one of those entrepreneurs who rushes around being busy but achieving no results, consider the difference between hard work and smart work, between activity and productivity.

Long hours are wasteful if you are not doing the right work. So focus on the appropriate priorities all of the time, every week, every minute. No matter how many hours you are willing to work, time is still finite. Make comprehensive lists of everything you need to do. Then choose the tasks that simply have to be done.

At the start of a week, ask yourself: "What is the most valuable work I should be doing?" At the start of every day, ask yourself the same question: "What is the most valuable work I must do today?"

Consider the difference between urgency and importance. Say a potential customer and a potential supplier both send you emails to say that they must speak to you urgently. Both seem urgent. But which one is important? Responding to which one will make the bigger difference to your business?

Stop yourself every time any new task interrupts what you are doing. Ask yourself whether it is truly important or merely urgent. Importance should trump urgency every time. Look at the matrix below and seek to do the important/urgent first, followed by the important/non-urgent. Don't allow yourself to be pushed in the wrong directions by tasks that are urgent but not important.

Focus on one task at a time. Get the most important one done before moving on to the next. Avoid getting fragmented, becoming distracted by a second or third task before the first is completed. Be disciplined with yourself in prioritizing and then ruthlessly completing what absolutely must be done.

Table 2

		High Importance	Low Importance
Urgency	High	1. Important and urgent – do these immediately	3. Urgent but not important – do these eventually
	Low	2. Important but not urgent – do these next	4. Not urgent and unimportant – ignore these entirely

Consider the alternative

Entrepreneurs are very action-oriented – sometimes a little too action-oriented for their own good.

The most successful entrepreneurs take the time to evaluate situations and consider options. They don't dawdle, but they hold themselves back for long enough to make sure they have enough information. Rather than asking themselves *what* the best way to do something is, they ask themselves *why* this issue has arisen in the first place. Is fixing the problem merely tackling a symptom or the root cause of the issue? How could the problem be prevented from recurring rather than dealing with it this time and then having to deal with it again and again in the future? This goes back to that difference between doing lots of work and the right work, of throwing yourself into a solution and holding yourself back to consider the best solution.

When it comes time to act, canny entrepreneurs again stop to think. They brainstorm alternatives rather than jump straight into the fray. Even if you are working on your own with no employees, take the time to think of at least three different ways to tackle a problem. If you get stuck, consider what your favorite entrepreneurial role model would do in your situation. Would they deal with it themselves, get help in, or ignore it entirely?

Entrepreneurs like action, and action is commendable. But learn first to evaluate a situation and weigh up different options to make sure you are spending your time on the right solution.

Keep negative emotions at bay

Here's the bad news: it won't all be plain sailing. Assumptions you've made in your plan won't pan out, suppliers may deliver the wrong goods, customers will change their mind and let you down. And it's natural to worry. Whether you are about to go into a meeting, merely sitting at your desk, or lying in bed at night, fears may rear up in your mind and derail your thoughts. While it's natural to worry, there's often no point doing it. It doesn't accomplish anything, it just makes you feel bad and stops you from being productive.

It goes without saying that it's easier said than done not to worry. Here are some practical tips for keeping those harmful emotions at bay:

- Write down what is worrying you. Spend a good 5, 10, or 15 minutes writing down what your worries are and how it makes you feel. The process usually helps the rational bit of your brain to get it into perspective and calm you down.
- Figure out the actions you will take to sort out the source of your concern. If a customer hasn't turned up, make a decision as to how long you will wait before giving them a ring, then move on and do something else. Keep a notepad by your bed so you can get must-do actions out of your head at night and onto paper to deal with the next day.
- Practice blanking out your mind. Sit quietly for a few minutes, close your eyes and think of nothing. Monitor your internal dialog – that voice in your head – and make sure it is absolutely quiet. If you catch the little voice drifting onto your concerns or wondering what time it is or speaking at all, make an effort to throttle it back. Do it for five or ten minutes, letting your body go slack and the tension easing from your muscles. You'll feel much better afterwards.

- Talk to someone about the source of your worry.
  Whether it's a colleague, a friend, or even a partner at
  home, share your thoughts and feelings. You may find
  that you don't even need their advice. The mere act of
  telling someone about your worries will often alleviate
  some of the negative feelings and allow you to get on
  with what you need to do.

- Practice what you need to do. If you are worried about
  an important meeting, presentation, or task you need
  to perform, use the time to rehearse whatever you need
  to do. Perhaps practice what you will say out loud.
  Role-play it through with a colleague. Visualize exactly
  what you plan to do in your mind's eye. Take whatever
  steps you need to feel more comfortable with the
  challenge ahead.

06

Selling and Making Money

When you open your doors to business, customers will not be ready with cash to spend, clients will not be logging on to snap up your shipments, the telephone will not ring itself. Whether you are building a retail store, an online business, or a service business, you must sell.

No matter how good your product, it will not sell itself.

Success is not an entitlement; it is something that has to be earned through marketing, promotion, and putting your offering in front of customers. This section covers everything you need to do to make you, your customers, and your bottom line happy.

Some of the tips here are more appropriate for some types of businesses than others. But whatever you do, the notion of selling should be ingrained into you, your business, your employees, and everything you do.

Get out there and sell.

Understand the importance of selling

I recommend to you, ambitious entrepreneur, that if you

can only get one thing right, get the selling right. There are far too many people who are great at what they do, but can't find a customer to pay for it. Of course you are going to be excited by your new product or freshly launched service, but if you can't get enough customers to pay you for it, you'll either need to sell harder or change what you offer.

On the other hand, there are plenty of businesses that thrive selling mediocre or downright shoddy goods and services. I better not name them or I'll get my ass sued off, but if they can succeed with only passable offerings, think how well you might do if you could get the selling right for the (hopefully) great offering you have.

Perhaps the second most important word after selling is "target." If you don't know how much you need to sell every week or month to make money, you're going to be in trouble. Sell too much and you can always hire people to make and deliver the product or service; fail to sell and your business has no future. A business without customers is no business at all. The secret to successful enterprise really is that simple.

Sell, sell, sell

I used to be a wage slave for a small consultancy. The firm's sales were static so the partners in the business decided to do some marketing. They spent many hours and many meetings writing brochures; they spent many more hours and many more meetings designing the brochures; they spent a small fortune printing them on glossy card and sending them to potential clients. But it didn't pick up a single client. Not one. Because the partners had confused marketing with selling.

Here's what I mean. Marketing raises your profile. It lets customers know what you offer. But unless you get lucky, the chances are that your customer will quickly move on and forget you.

People handing out leaflets on the street, people stuffing pamphlets through your letter box, pop-up windows when you are surfing the web, those are marketing tools. And I'll bet you don't respond to those very often.

However, offering free ice-cream samples on the street, pointing out the natural flavors, handing out a voucher for a buy-one, get-one free offer, and then personally guiding interested customers back to the shop – that's selling. Following up a marketing brochure with a phone call, an email, another phone call, yet another, and then a meeting – that's selling.

If marketing is letting customers know what you offer, selling is showing them the value of what you offer.

Print brochures, leaflets, newsletters, or pamphlets only if you must. I'm quite serious about this. Realize though that they will capture potential customers' attentions for mere seconds, if at all. To sell, you must engage with your customers, challenge them to think, give them the chance to try your product or service. A brochure will never impress a customer, but you might. Only then will you get them to pay for what you do and turn your business into a success.

Focus on serving, not selling

Selling has a bad reputation and, in many cases, rightly so. Pushy sales people are often more interested in making you part with your money than in providing you with a useful service or product.

But that kind of sales technique only ever works once on a customer. Push a product on trusting customers that they don't need and, well, they are hardly likely to come back. Even the most gullible customer learns surprisingly quickly.

The secret of good sales practice is providing a useful service. Helping customers to understand the benefits you provide before they buy. Ensuring they experience those benefits once they have bought. Even pointing out that what you do is not right for them if that's the case. You may lose a customer in the short term, but you will have gained an advocate, someone who will endorse you and boast about you to their colleagues and contacts.

The same goes for what you do behind the scenes as well as in front of the customer. Lots of businesses focus on cost, more specifically, on cutting costs and on providing a service as easily and cheaply as possible. However, that can be short-sighted. Rip off a customer and you will lose a customer. Instead, ask yourself: Is this how you would want to be treated if you were your own customer?

Whether you are chasing a handful of corporate customers a month or hundreds of customers a day, the rules are still the same. Focus on building a rapport, offering a service that truly benefits the customers, and keeping them happy.

Mention benefits, not features

Features tell customers what your offering is; benefits tell customers why they should buy it. Whether you are selling in person or over the telephone, through a website, a brochure, or a written proposal, spend your time emphasizing the benefits of what you offer, not its features.

Here's an example: "We are a city-wide business with 13 branches" is a feature. But how does that help your customer? Answer: It doesn't. But "Having 13 branches means we can guarantee delivery to your business within 45 minutes of any order" tells the feature and sells the benefit.

"All of our food is sourced from an organic farm in Italy" is a feature, but "Our food tastes better than any packaged meal you can buy" is a benefit.

"Our printer cartridges are refillable" could confuse a customer who is not technically minded. "The cost of running our printers is roughly half that of running a conventional printer" is a clear benefit.

If you can't figure out the benefits of your own offering, list each of its features and ask yourself: "Why should that be interesting?" "So what?"

And make sure you use your customers' language, not your own. Because, let's get this straight, if they misunderstand you, it's your fault, not theirs. Choose your words and phrases carefully and avoid jargon and TLAs (three letter abbreviations) unless it's terminology you are sure they want you to talk about.

Perhaps you have already heard this advice before. Talk benefits, not features. And choose language that your customers know and use. But why is it then that so few entrepreneurs actually do it? Perhaps they get carried away with the technical specifications of what they have spent so long devising and bringing to market. Perhaps they think that their customers are different. You must understand that your customers do not care about features, they want only to know how it will benefit them, make them feel good, or salve some form of pain away.

Ask and listen before you tell and sell

On the topic of selling, someone older and wiser once reminded me that I have one mouth and two ears – and should use them in that ratio. Beware of throwing a long list of your product's benefits at your customers. That's the kind of tactic that a pushy sales person might use. No, you are going to take a different approach. You will ask questions and establish your customer's wants and needs first, and mention only the benefits that are relevant to him or her.

Imagine each and every one of your customers has a big sticker on their foreheads saying: "What will this do for me?" Big emphasis on the "me." Everyone wants to be treated as an individual, not just another customer. Make an assumption based on their similarity to other customers and you will almost certainly offend them.

Establish before you meet customers what the best open-ended questions would be. If you have an hour-long meeting with a customer, you may well need dozens of questions to establish their needs – whether it's for their organization, their family, or themselves. If you only have

30 seconds while selling them a muffin or an item of clothing, just a couple of questions may be all you can realistically ask. Plan what you can say to different customers rather than risk making the wrong impact.

Even a simple question such as "How are you today?" may elicit a useful response. Sure, most customers may respond with a standard "Fine" or "Good, thanks," but others will reveal what they want – "I'm in a real rush today, I need to buy a present but don't know what to get" or "I'm so hot, I could really do with a long, refreshing, ice-cold drink" or "I'm a bit stressed to be honest, we are pitching for a new account tomorrow and I only have 30 minutes for this meeting if that's OK with you."

Ask a question, listen to their response. Try to understand their point of view, their problems, concerns or issues, and opportunities. Only then should you mention a relevant feature and go into its benefit. And then repeat as necessary.

Understand that people like people like them

Remember that business is all about people and relationships. No matter how dazzling or technically superior your offering, your customers are buying from you or your team. It's a case of people buying from people.

Human beings have been gathering themselves in tribes and gangs for thousands of years. They burned symbols and scratched markings into their flesh to indicate membership of one tribe rather than another. Even today, members of street gangs distinguish themselves from other factions by their clothing and hairstyles, tattoos and piercings, language and jargon.

It is in the deepest part of human nature for people to like people who are like themselves. People within an organization tend to dress alike, speak alike, think alike. Friends tend to buy from the same shops, eat at similar restaurants, drive cars in the same price range. People within a group always deny the similarity; they lack the objectivity to see it for themselves. But you can exploit this effect to encourage your customers to buy from you.

Whether you sell online, in print, or in person, think about how to connect with your audience. Perhaps it's through sarcasm and profanity for hip 18- to 24-year-olds, an emphasis on the miracle of life for mothers-to-be, or wild-eyed enthusiasm and a mass of statistics for sports aficionados.

Think even about how you dress and groom yourself. If you're selling burgers on a building site or setting up an exclusive bistro in the most expensive part of town, go to lengths to blend in. If you're visiting a media firm that describes itself as young and funky, ditch the suit and throw on those designer jeans.

Remember that people like people like them, and liking is only a short step away from buying.

Press the flesh

Communication. There are many technological ways to communicate, but people have been trading and transacting in person since the dawn of humanity. Even relatively low-tech methods of communication such as the postal service are only a couple of hundred years old. Touch trumps tech every time.

Think how many emails you get every day. A busy customer probably gets ten times as many. Even a valuable email that engages and educates an existing customer could accidentally get deleted with the mere click of a mouse. A secretary could easily bin an important letter or brochure without realizing it. And the direct marketing (or "junk mail" to you and me) industry aims to produce a 2 percent hit rate. Which, it does not take a genius to conclude, isn't very high at all.

Firing off an email is going to win you less business than sending a handwritten letter. A letter is still less effective than an instant message exchange. Better still is a phone call when a customer can hear your voice, ask questions, interact with you. But nothing beats a face-to-face meeting, when you can look each other in the eyes and be each other's sole focus of attention.

It's easy to keep busy, to sit at your desk and type 200 individually crafted emails to potential customers, to spend hours making dozens of phone calls. It's more difficult to ensure you are productive rather than merely busy. A single meeting a day may win you more business than hours of phone calls, letter writing, and emails combined.

Make sure you get out and about and face-to-face with your customers. Set yourself a target and make it a priority to go to a number of networking events every month. Customers are much more likely to buy when they can ask questions, hear the excitement in your voice, and watch your body language exuding conviction.

Every time you send off an email, tell your customer that you will follow it up with a phone call. When you manage to speak, propose meeting up to understand a little more about your customer and their need. Keep moving away from the high-tech and low-touch. Secure that contact and press the flesh.

Promote, sell, and promote some more

When the order book looks lean, when the shop seems a bit quiet, when your employees are surfing the internet to kill time, it's time to get out and jump-start sales again.

Marketing and selling are not activities that you do and then stop. You need to keep marketing and selling, marketing and selling and, even when you think you have done enough, do some more marketing and selling. Think in terms of a campaign of ongoing action rather than a one-off event. Successful selling should stop only slightly short of stalking!

If you can't seem to get face to face with your customers, try something different. Change your tactics, mix up your tricks.

If you are sitting in the office and wondering what to do next, pick up the telephone. Fire off an email. Pick up a pen and write a letter for a change. If one mailing doesn't work, do another, and another. Create a new angle, tap into a new taste or trend or worry. Try something different.

Get in touch with existing customers and chase for

appointments and introductions, referrals and leads. Offer to give a talk, run a seminar, conduct a half-day workshop. Have something new to say, invite yourself over to their offices because you "happen to be in the area." Suggest a breakfast meeting, a coffee meeting, lunch at a classy restaurant, a shared sandwich at the shop across the street, a drink after work. Never finish any conversation with a customer promising to get back in touch with you – he or she won't. Always tell the customer how you will be in touch next.

Beyond that, open the phone book or a business directory and call up a business and make them an offer. Your timing could be just right and you might pick up a new customer.

If you run a shop or restaurant, take your wares onto the streets. Get permission from your town council to set up a stall on the pavement to show off your goods. If you run a hairdressing salon, set up a temporary hairdressing station in a busy street and give someone a haircut for free. If you run a car showroom, park one of your cars in a public square and invite passers-by to get into the driving seat. Hire commissioned sales reps, strike deals with other companies to become resellers. Think of ways to create strategic alliances; offer to exchange floor space, shelf space, or web space with a complementary retailer or service provider. Propose that customers can have a full refund if they aren't entirely happy.

What else could you do?

Persist, persist, persist

Much worse than overselling to a customer is underselling.

I'm sure you can think of good reasons not to put more work into selling. You may feel that your product is so exceptional that it should sell itself. Then there's the effort involved, the minor indignity of having to talk to customers, the potential awkwardness of rejection.

But ponder on it a little more. Good things do not come to those who wait. Build it and they will not come – they come to those who make them happen. Impatience and persistence are very much qualities when it comes to making money.

Overselling means a customer might feel slightly irritated. At worst, customers who are fed up of being sold to will ignore your emails, stop returning your calls, maybe tell you to stop bothering them. Is that really so bad? They are not going to send trained assassins after you or kidnap your children to make you stop.

On the other hand, underselling means customers do not understand quite what you do or why it would be of benefit. Customers have short memories and underselling might mean they have forgotten you. Underselling may mean you no longer have a viable business. All in all, it's a bad, bad thing.

It is far better to pester a little too often than have customers forget you or not understand what you do.

Set yourself a sales goal

Not everyone enjoys selling, and if you struggle to motivate yourself, try this simple tip: Write down a set of sales goals. Here's why.

Back in the 1950s, researchers asked graduates from Harvard University whether they had any goals. As you would expect, almost all of them had goals. But only 3 percent of them actually wrote them down. Fast forward 30 years to a follow-up survey and, amazingly, the 3 percent who had put pen to paper had amassed as much wealth as the other 97 percent put together.

Tempted to write any sales goals down yet?

Writing it down helps to crystalize your intentions. It cements your goals and provides a visible reminder that you need to get on. It kicks you into action and makes you ten times more likely to do it.

It works for me. I know that if I write a list and keep it on my desk, I'll work furiously hard until I cross everything off it. On days I don't write lists, I don't get as much done. It goes without saying that I write a lot of lists.

This works for lots of activities and tasks, not just selling. If you put off doing your stock taking or bookkeeping or reading the small print in contracts or chasing up invoices, write yourself a goal to do it. Write down whatever you want to achieve tomorrow or the next week and stick it in a prominent place.

Start small when it comes to setting sales goals. Begin by calling just five or ten customers or spending a single hour on the street handing out free samples or doing whatever you need to do for your business. At the end of the day you'll find it was pretty straightforward. So set your goal for a bit more the next day, and still more the day after that.

Of course your goals have to be achievable. Sending personalized letters to 120 customers or picking up the phone to 80 customers in a day might be possible. But aiming for a 50 percent success rate in setting up appointments – that's out of your control. No one could guarantee that and you will only disappoint yourself. What I can guarantee is that little is more satisfying than crossing that last item off your list!

Push your prices up, up, up

If it costs more, it must be better, right?

If a business charges 50 percent more than its nearest competitor, it must have near mystical powers to rejuvenate its clients. Or if one fragrance costs twice as much as another, then its claim to have extracted oils from only the finest Himalayan orchid blossoms and Tunisian neroli must be true.

Price and quality are inextricably linked in the minds of most customers. Price yourself low and customers worry that you can't be any good. Price yourself high and you may become more exclusive, more expert, more of a draw.

Competing by offering the lowest price is not really competition at all. Most customers prioritize quality over the lowest prices and, sooner or later, someone else will figure out a way to do it cheaper. Look at your competitors and compare your pricing with theirs. If a competitor is charging more than you, is it really because they are smarter, faster, tastier, fresher, friendlier?

Strangely, businesses occasionally benefit when they push their prices up, reporting that they lose some customers but gain others. They may lose some of the undesirable customers, the kind that take a long time to make up their mind and worry about the little money they do have to spend. But they attract a rarer breed of better customer, the kind for whom quality is more important than price, excellence more important than saving pennies. Their volumes sometimes decrease but their profitability improves.

There are no guarantees, but play with your pricing. Have the confidence to experiment. Offer a product line at the back of the shop that costs ten times more than what you offer at the front, or try it the other way around. Suggest a fee to a new corporate customer that is twice what you have tried to charge in the past. If you boosted your prices by 10 percent or even 100 percent, what's the best that might happen?

Speak up and be noticed

Conference organizing is an industry in itself. Even as you read this sentence, there is probably an event going on somewhere discussing anything from retail trends and Asian entrepreneurs to manufacturing sector efficiency and advances in wireless technology. Every one of these events requires a handful of speakers who can communicate confidently and engagingly to the audience. Could that be you?

Becoming a speaker is an incredible way of building the profile for your business. Even though I am a psychologist,

I have spoken at events aimed at groups as diverse as IT managers, marketing types, and accountants.

All you need is to find a unique angle on the topic or main issues being discussed at the event. Think of your audience and answer their biggest question: "What's in it for me?" Perhaps you can share sector-specific knowledge, practical advice about the travails of founding a business, or even inspiration about succeeding in the face of adversity. There are many viewpoints to take on your experience and expertise; think laterally about it.

As a conference speaker, you have a distinct advantage when networking with delegates at the event. You can be confident that you can approach anyone, introduce yourself as a speaker, and find out what has drawn them to attend this event. It's the ultimate networking icebreaker, and one that will undoubtedly win you important new contacts and possibly even business.

Look for targeted media opportunities

Having a media profile rocks. I've written or been quoted in publications ranging from *Automotive Management* and *Accountancy* to *Cosmopolitan* and *Men's Health*. Not only has it been fun seeing my name in print, but it grabs the customers' attention too.

Customers can't buy from you unless they know you exist. The media can play a role in helping you share your message, raise your profile and, hopefully, bring more customers to you.

First figure out the angle to take. In much the same

way you draw people in with an elevator pitch, you need to decide how to whet the appetite of a journalist to cover what you have to say. Perhaps you are telling a tale of how you have overcome uncommon adversity to set up your outfit. Maybe you have an offering that has a unique flavor or unusual approach. Above all, think about what a reader might be interested in – what you want to tell the world may not be what they want to hear.

Next, choose the right media channel. Is your story significant enough to compete against world affairs on a television program? Is your story something that would suit a nationwide audience in a national newspaper, a professional audience in the trade press or on a specialist website, or perhaps a local audience in a local newspaper?

Journalists need good stories to plump up their pages or fill airtime; the worst they can say is no. And no is a word that, as an entrepreneur, you should be accustomed to hearing by now. On the other hand, think of the opportunities if they were to say yes.

Count the hits, not the misses

Misses are good. With every miss you learn something new. How do you think an Olympic gymnast learns to do a double back flip? By doing lots of single back flips and landing in an ungainly fashion, a bit off center, even on their butt, but eventually they get it right. They go on to try the double back flip and end up in a pile of limbs on the floor all over again. But then they land one perfectly and perhaps after more practice another and another.

If you call on a customer and get turned away, you have learned what does not work. After a while, you learn to change your sales spiel. A customer comes into your shop to browse but goes away without making a purchase. Next time you will change your patter or arrange your counter display a little differently.

Not even the best sales people in the world hit the mark every time. The best sales people differentiate themselves from the rest because they pick themselves up and carry on regardless. The average sales people wonder and worry. The top sales people learn what they can, put the misses down to experience, and carry on anyway.

Become an implant

If selling is about spending time with potential customers, it should follow that spending more time with customers should lead to more sales.

If you have corporate customers, get out of your office and try working at their premises. Implant yourself into their business. Ask for an empty meeting room or even a desk in their open-plan area. Even if you are just doing research or writing reports that you could do from your own office or your home, use it as an opportunity to raise your profile. Remind your customer that you exist. Not for nothing does the old adage say that if you're out of sight, you're out of mind.

Your physical presence not only reminds your customers that you exist, it also encourages them to ask you questions, perhaps share a joke with you, and cement the relationship a little more, treat you like a member of the team. It allows you to absorb snippets of information about their culture as well as observe further opportunities with which to get involved.

Becoming an implant isn't just limited to office-based entrepreneurs. Of course there are hairdressers, acupuncturists, and sports massage therapists who come away from their salons and clinics to visit their corporate clients. Coffee powerhouse Starbucks have managed to implant themselves inside retailers such as Border and Esprit. Sandwich chains such as Pret A Manger offer to come to you to cater for office lunches and dinners. Software companies are happy to send their people over to provide free training seminars or run helpdesks. So what is stopping you from offering your equivalent?

Charge up your customer conveyor belt

Back in my wage slave days, when I used to work for other bosses in a consultancy, we used to go from feast to famine, famine to feast, and back again. We either had so much work that everyone was exhausted or so little work that the bosses would threaten us with redundancy.

Never allow yourself to get complacent serving existing customers. Sure, it's a great feeling when you have a few customers and you start to get busy, but in all likelihood one of your customers will find another supplier, cease to need you, or go out of business. Whatever the reason, customers come and go. As you lose some, you must have new ones to not only replace them but also grow the business. Make it a priority to juggle the tasks of serving existing customers with finding new ones.

Organizations often talk about managing a sales pipeline or fueling a sales funnel, but I like the analogy of a creaky old conveyor belt. Stick 20 contacts and potential buyers on at one end of the conveyor belt and as the buyers roll down the juddering and bumpy belt, some fall off. Perhaps they lose interest or decide they can't afford it, a few more fall off because they say yes and suddenly change their mind or get poached by a competitor. Only a few get to your end, the end where they agree to pay you for what you do.

Monitor your customer conveyor belt on a regular basis to ensure that your orders are not suddenly going to dry up. Bear in mind that contacts can take a long time to come towards you on the conveyor belt. And they do not move simply of their own accord. Quite the opposite: If you forget to tend to the machine, your potential customers slip backwards, away. Track their progress and take appropriate steps to keep that conveyor belt moving. Keep grabbing their attention and keep deepening your understanding of their needs and their understanding of you.

The second you feel settled and content that you have enough business is probably the moment it could all go wrong. Unless you are actively seeking new contacts to put on the far end of your sales conveyor belt, you risk having no customers sometime soon. Keep cranking that conveyor belt handle.

Create customer delight

A single sale is like the first step of dating; what you're hoping for is that the date will turn into another and another and eventually a relationship. In business, it's relationships, not a succession of one-night stands, that will help you flourish.

Finding new customers all of the time is simply too much hard work. It is far easier to look after your existing customers so they return time and again. This is because – and this'll get your attention – the bottom line is that ongoing customer relationships are much more profitable than individual customer transactions.

Everyone likes something for nothing. I bought a birthday card recently and got given a free chocolate bar. When I bought a lamp I got a free energy-saving bulb. It's often these little favors that stick in your mind.

Surprise your customers and offer more than they paid for. Do it sporadically, unexpectedly, or else they'll expect it all of the time. Deliver the document to them a week early. Send a car to pick a customer up or offer them a branded umbrella to take home on a rainy day. Offer a free manicure to go with their spa treatment. Suggest a pair of shoes from the store across the street that would go with their new dress. Send over a free drink "on the house." Give them a free tester to take away. Throw in 20 percent more than they paid for.

If you have a relatively small number of big-spending customers, try phoning them after they have made a purchase. Ask if they are enjoying your product or service, check if they are having any teething problems, and offer to talk them through the functions on the phone or in person. If there's a hint of a doubt or worry or problem, take immediate steps to sort it out for them. Even if you have to offer a total refund, you may be surprised at how many customer referrals come from initially unhappy customers.

It goes back to the principle of serving rather than selling. Treasure your customers as human beings rather than mere buyers. The moment a customer has paid should never be the end of a transaction but the start of a relationship.

Make it a top-notch customer experience and you will see your customer return again and bring friends or colleagues too next time.

Categorize your customers

What do property, peapods, and Italian economists have to do with your customers?

Quite a lot, as it turns out. Vilfredo Pareto was a nineteenth-century Italian economist and philosopher who first identified that 80 percent of the property in Italy was owned by only 20 percent of the population. He later noticed that 80 percent of the pea harvest in his garden was produced by around 20 percent of his peapods. And so came Pareto's Principle, the 80/20 rule, or the rule of the vital few and the trivial many.

When it comes down to your customers, not all of them are of equal worth. If you run a sandwich shop, you may notice a few faces who come in every day, week after week, month after month. Perhaps you run an interior design business and have noticed that the residents of a particular district are responsible for giving you the majority of your referrals. Or as a corporate consultant, you notice that a handful of your customers generate more revenue than the rest put together.

Essentially, 80 percent of your income will come from only 20 percent of your customers. With some careful analysis, you might find that the ratio in your business is actually 70/30 or 67.2/32.8. But the precise numbers aren't what matter. What matters is that a small number of your customers will provide you with most of your earnings. Which should tell you who to spend your time with, paying those customers special attention, and ensuring they return again and again.

Take a look at your customer base. Identify who the big spenders are. And focus on them, cherish them, look after them. Because the moment you take their loyalty for granted is when they might just get itchy feet and start to look around at your competitors.

But don't stop there, take your analysis further. Ask yourself a simple question: what's different? Understand how your big spenders differ from the rest of your customers. Are there common characteristics that stand out amongst your key customers? Do they have similar backgrounds or issues? Is there perhaps a particular product or service line you offer that is more attractive than the rest? Or is it that you behave differently when dealing with those customers? If you can understand why these customers are your most important customers, you can focus your efforts on attracting the right sort of new customers.

Ask for referrals

Word of mouth kicks ass. There can be no other way to put it. Get a customer to evangelize willingly about you to other people and you are on to a winning (and profitable) formula. But sometimes customers need a little encouraging to help you spread the word.

Perhaps it is shyness or embarrassment that stops many entrepreneurs from asking for referrals. Sure you would prefer your service to be so good that customers want to spread the word without prompting. Maybe you feel that it is even a little impolite to ask – but it isn't. Customers are busy people and even if they love what you do for them, it may simply not occur to them to recommend you to others.

If you are confident that your offering to customers is strong, you should have the confidence to ask for referrals. Of course asking a dissatisfied customer for a referral is adding insult to injury, but why would a happy customer not be open-minded about sharing good news with the people they know?

A corporate buyer will undoubtedly have contacts in other organizations, perhaps competitors or previous employers. A consumer will have friends, family, and colleagues who might enjoy and benefit from what you offer.

Gathering referrals is an incredibly low-cost method of generating new business. So invest in making it happen. Encourage further referrals by thanking the customers who do refer you. Show your appreciation not only in words but perhaps with a discount voucher, a bottle of champagne, a weekend break. If they are not allowed to accept personal gifts, offer a pile of business books, tickets to a business seminar, or a free trial of a new product of yours.

One final word of caution, though. A gift after you have gathered a referral is called a thank you. A gift offered before a referral might be constituted as a bribe. Tread carefully.

07

Hiring People

You may need to believe in yourself to succeed, but the moment you believe you can do it all or are infallible ... well, I'm sure you can guess how that will turn out. So surround yourself with good people.

The quality of your customer experience ultimately depends on the caliber of your people. The plushest office, the flashiest website, the most exceptional store won't matter if customers walk in or telephone in and get treated gruffly or incompetently by an employee.

In keeping with the theme of the book, this short section is not about the legalities of hiring or the technicalities of employment contracts; you can always appoint a lawyer or a human resources person to sort those out for you. Instead, I'm going to share with you the most important rules for hiring the right kind of people and creating a culture that will help your business to grow and succeed.

Hire for temperament, not qualifications

Skills can be taught, motivation can't. If you have

people who are enthusiastic and motivated, you can teach them most skills. They will practice and ask for advice, take on board your comments, and try to improve. However, if they are unmotivated, you may struggle to get them to demonstrate even the skills they already have.

Qualifications are overrated. Someone graduated top of their class at university or secretarial college, a culinary academy, or a top business school, but what does that really tell you? All it tells you is that this person is good at exams. When looking for people to bring into your team, ask lots of questions about their motivation, their work ethic, their persistence and determination.

Don't just ask, "Are you a motivated person?" because only the most dim-witted of candidates is likely to say no. Instead, ask for specific examples in which the person has demonstrated commitment to getting a job done. Don't let the candidate speak in general terms. Ask about specific incidents and get them to tell you how the situation arose, exactly what they did, and what the result was. Try some of these:

- "Can you tell me about a time when you had to work really hard to get something done?"
- "Can you tell me about a time when you had to motivate yourself to finish a job?"
- "Give me an example of a situation in which you persevered in the face of adversity to get something done."
- "Tell me about a time you had to go above and beyond the call of duty."

• "Can you tell me about a time when you exceeded a customer's expectations?"

You will know good candidates when you meet them. They give examples and stories that astound you with their tenacity and willingness to put their work ahead of everything else; they make other candidates look downright idle. Look for people who are motivated and you will never have to worry about motivating them.

Place a premium on people skills

You've probably heard of the term EQ – emotional intelligence – unless you just landed from Mars. Plenty of research shows that emotional intelligence beats traditional rocket scientist measures of intelligence at predicting success at work. Unless your new venture is trying to launch rockets into outer space, of course.

Customers buy from an outfit when they like the people who run it, so make sure you hire people who have empathy, natural warmth, optimism and self-awareness. Even if you are hiring employees who will not deal with customers, bear in mind they still have to deal, liaise, and communicate with other members of the team every day.

In practical terms, that means looking for people who can empathize with the plight of other people. Ask them how they felt when situations went wrong at work or when a colleague got disciplined for poor work. If they sneer at others less good than themselves, is that the kind of person you want in your team?

Ask them to tell you about their own strengths and weaknesses. Push them to be candid about the areas in which they need to develop. Ask about the last time they got criticized and how they responded to it. Of course they will be guarded about their weaknesses, but if they feel they don't have any, are they really claiming that they are perfect? To me, someone who says that they have never been criticized and believes that they are faultless is deeply, very deeply, flawed.

Ask about prior success

Whatever the skills you are looking for, ask candidates to tell you about similar situations they have handled in the past. Avoid at all costs asking how they think they would handle the situation if it ever arose.

I'll say it again. Ask questions about real incidents that happened to them in the past. Steer clear of questions that ask them how they would handle hypothetical future situations.

Put it another way. Ask questions that get them to talk in the past tense, not the future tense.

I apologize for hammering it home, but even when I've explained it to interviewers in person, they still struggle to put it into practice, drifting into "How would you...?" (bad) rather than "How did you...?" (good) questions.

This one is important. Because there is compelling research to indicate that the best predictor of future success is past behavior. Someone who has demonstrated a skill in the past will almost always be better at it than someone who has never done it before. A candidate who has sold to customers in the past will be better at it than another who has only studied the theory. An applicant who has coped with the pressure of too much work will cope better with it in the future than another who merely thinks he or she knows how to prioritize and get a job done.

If you ask a question about how someone might handle a situation, even someone who has no experience of handling that situation will typically be able to cobble together a response that sounds fairly sensible.

Now that I've mentioned it, it probably seems startlingly obvious. But I've observed interviewers in businesses ranging from law firms and investment banks to retailers and technology companies making this mistake. Of asking about hypothetical future situations rather than actual situations that the candidates had been in. For the sake of your business, please do not fall into the same trap.

Pay well, reward better

We all need money to pay the rent, buy food and clothes, maybe even go on holiday once in a while. But the astute entrepreneur knows to reward people with more than just money.

Of course you need to offer market rates in respect of basic salary, commission, bonuses, overtime, and benefits to attract candidates' attention. However, paying well is not just about money. It is about paying with challenge and responsibility, courtesy and respect. It is about figuring out the right buttons for each of your employees and pushing them until they can't imagine working elsewhere.

Don't get into a bidding war with your competitors over pay. If you have employees who are only sticking with you because you are able to pay a few more pennies an hour, you should not worry unduly about losing them. Look to catch the attention of employees who want to join you because they really want the job.

Focus on the nature of the work, the fun, the opportunity. Give your employees the chance to make decisions and influence the direction of the business. Offer training and development opportunities that are second to none. Surprise the team by buying a cake and closing the office one Friday afternoon to celebrate a team achievement. Agree to flexible hours, casual office wear, and time off during a quiet week as a thank you for working crazy hours the week before. Let the work speak for itself and look for people who are genuinely excited to join you on your entrepreneurial journey.

Remember that this is your business. You are the boss! You do not have to adopt any business practice simply because it goes on elsewhere. Think of your own special ways to make your working environment interesting, stimulating, and worthwhile. Use everything and anything you can think of to keep good people working for you rather than somebody else.

08

Evolving and Advancing the Business

At some stage you will suddenly realize that you are running a business. No longer are you setting up or struggling to find customers – you have a flow of customers, some of them regular, some of them not so regular. The business is bringing in enough sales to cover your costs and hopefully you are even able to take some profit out of the business.

And so we reach the end of the entrepreneurial journey. Or do we? Entrepreneurs who think they have "made it" are almost certainly looking for trouble.

The world of business does not stand still. Like the seasons, your customers' tastes and needs are ever changing. Fickle customers get bored, look for new experiences, and move on. Competitors put out new products and services to lure your customers away. New players enter the market and turn entire industries on their head and, with new technologies and increasingly sophisticated customers, the pace of change will only quicken.

If you continue only to do what you have already been doing, you will notice the world moving swiftly away from you. Business requires a constant push at making your company more efficient, more effective, more customer-focused. To turn your fledgling enterprise into a burgeoning one, you must force your business to evolve.

Grow or grow

You have no choice; if you want to succeed and have a long-term future running the business, you must decide to grow either in size or professionally.

Many businesses look to grow in size, adding further branches, offices, shops, clinics, salons, restaurants, or whatever. Once they are happy with their format or offering, the owners look to hire more people, grow revenues, and increase the size of the business until they can perhaps sell the business (and make lots of money) or float the business (and make lots of money).

The other alternative is to stay the same size, but offer new services and products to keep customers coming back to you. Perhaps you do not want the stress of having to oversee an increasingly large and sprawling business, maybe you would prefer to keep your enterprise small to balance your work and life. However, if your revenues are not growing at all, then in real terms you are getting worse off every year. Assuming you have good products or services, your competitors will undoubtedly try to imitate them, learn from them, find ways of offering them more quickly or cheaply. If you continue to offer only the same products and services, you will notice as the months go by that fewer of your regular customers will come back.

In the world of professional services, for example, the choice is often whether to grow and try for larger projects – perhaps moving from local to national and then international customers – or to stay a boutique, offering niche products to a very specialized market.

So make a decision as to how you wish to grow. Grow the size, scope, and scale of the business, or grow mentally, technically, professionally to offer leading-edge products and services to keep you ahead of your competitors.

Work in and on your business

Working in the business is doing whatever needs attention to keep the business running today. *Working on the business* is thinking about its future.

If you run a travel agency, working in the business probably includes taking telephone calls, printing off tickets, posting tickets to customers, greeting customers who come in through the door and selling them holidays, answering emails, calling hotels to ask about availability, taking still more customer calls, paying bills, juggling yet another customer who has walked in with yet more customer calls, cleaning the office, restocking the shelves with brochures, and getting it locked up at night.

Working on the business is planning its future, reviewing customer comments and tweaking the service, examining the market for threats and opportunities, deciding on new products to develop or services to launch, advertising to find good candidates and interviewing them to decide who to bring on board, investigating training courses for yourself, cultivating an appetite for learning in the rest of the team, and looking for ways to grow and thrive and succeed.

Work in your business to ensure you do whatever needs doing to ensure the business can make it to the next week or month. Work on your business to guarantee you still have a business next year and the year after that.

Some entrepreneurs are naturally better at working in the business than on it, of tackling immediate concerns rather than taking the long-term view. However, if you exhaust yourself working on the day-to-day, then the market, your competitors, and customers will move on. Other entrepreneurs are exactly the opposite – they are being drawn constantly by the lure of working on the future of the business rather than in it to get business done. If you spend too much time thinking about the big picture you could end up with not enough customers today to pay the bills. Work out which you are better at, and then work hard at doing the other.

Continue to exploit networks

A big part of continuing to work on your business, rather than merely in it, is to keep networking and to keep meeting a wide variety of people, talking ideas over, learning and looking for inspiration.

Go to conferences and dip into trade exhibitions. Keep paying fees to be a member of the relevant associations or industry groups. Never allow yourself to believe that you are too busy servicing current customer needs to keep an eye out on what else is going on in the marketplace. Spend too long looking inwards and you may well fail to spot the "next big thing" affecting your field.

You may no longer need external investors and feel that such events are insufficiently useful for picking up new customers, but networking is still a valuable tool for keeping an eye on issues and opportunities affecting the sector. You could learn anything from the latest on the government's plans to reform small business tax laws to news about new entrants into the market. Plus it's the perfect opportunity to check out what competitors are doing too.

Some entrepreneurs feel that there are no networks or associations that cover exactly what they do, they feel sidelined at some of the industry's big events and never feel able to learn enough to bother going. What's to stop you from setting up your own network, your own association, or informal group? Even if your group consists only of a half-dozen people meeting a couple of times a year to discuss common issues, you can gain so much from sharing your issues and listening to those of others.

You will learn more up-to-date and useful information from networking than you could ever read in a newspaper. You will end up filling hard-to-fill vacancies through recommendation. You may well solve your biggest problems through the ideas and insights of others.

Business is fundamentally about people and relationships. Always make time to connect and learn from others.

Keep your secrets safe

Not for nothing does the Coca-Cola company guard the formulation of its eponymous drink. Your secrets are your competitive edge. Share them and it could be game over.

People will flatter you and ask what your secret is. A supplier may enquire as to the secret of your success. A friend may wonder how you have grown your business. A journalist may want to write a piece on you. They may tell you how brilliant, innovative, and refreshing your business is, but don't give in. Simply smile and thank them for their praise.

By all means publicize your services and products but always think before you speak, and encourage your employees to do the same. Otherwise even a receptionist trying to be helpful could inadvertently reveal secrets that could wreck your business. Talk in general terms but conceal the names or dates, ingredients or other details that could lose you your competitive advantage.

The more valuable your secret, the more you should be willing to pay to keep it. Hire security specialists to encrypt your communications and lock down your computers. Seek legal guidance on protecting your intellectual property; apply for patents and trademarks, and copyright whatever you can. Give your employees the information they need to do their jobs but nothing more. Pay lawyers to put clauses into your employees' and suppliers' contracts to ensure they cannot sell your secrets to the highest bidder without dire personal consequences.

Safeguarding your secrets is often the secret of success.

Ask for a poke IN the eye

A business that is doing well can become complacent. Fact is, success makes entrepreneurs stupid.

An almost certain sign that a business is about to hit the rocks is the absence of customer complaints. Customers are never happy all of the time; they are either not being candid or not being contacted.

Ask your customers for feedback. Then listen and make appropriate changes to the business. Ask, ask, ask. Listen, listen, listen.

Listen even if you think what they are saying is stupid, tedious, obvious, and worthy of scorn. Respect that if they have cause to complain, there is usually reason for it. Perhaps it wasn't a problem with the product or service so much as the way it was sold to them or their having misunderstood it. No prizes for guessing whose job it is to fix it so future customers will be gloriously happy.

However, the whole business of feedback can be treacherous for the unwary. Numerous entrepreneurs fall into the trap of asking questions but only wanting to hear good news. The true entrepreneur knows to ask for the equivalent of a poke in the eye or a slap in the face by asking specifically for negative feedback. Ask where you underperform and invite your customers to compare your offering with those of your competitors. Ask for suggestions how your offering could be better. Enquire what is missing and what else they might want.

Bear in mind that customers dislike giving bad news in person. Customers hate to be negative when they have to look you in the eye or hear the disappointment in your voice. Whatever means of gathering feedback you employ, give customers the blanket of anonymity to tell you what they really think. Make sure they are free to be as honest as you need them to be:

- Invite customers to complete postage-paid forms.
- Leave a comments book in a corner of your shop or office reception.
- Employ a freelance market researcher to survey your customers by telephone.
- Get third-party interviewers to go meet your customers one-on-one. Avoid at all cost the cumbersome (and expensive) focus group.

Too many organizations make the gathering of feedback a laborious exercise. They focus too much on the research methodology, the choosing of respondents, the validity of the data. Keep it simple. All you need are the honest thoughts of your customers.

Keep questioning your customers

Feedback is valuable, you can never get enough of it. Any time you have a few minutes with customers, take the opportunity to ask a question or two, learn more about them, and figure out ways to serve them better.

Of course you should be careful not to bombard a customer with a long stream of questions. Two or three questions show your interest; too many more will feel intrusive. This should feel like a conversation, not an interrogation. Some questions may be appropriate for long-standing, returning customers; other questions may be appropriate for everyone.

In any case, here are some questions to prompt your thinking:

- How did you hear about us?
- Who else have you bought similar products from in the past?
- What did you like about their products?
- What did you dislike about their products?
- What are your other favorite suppliers/shops/restaurants/consultants/etc at the moment?
- What most annoys you about your other suppliers/shops/restaurants/consultants/etc?
- What do you think we could do to get your friends/colleagues to buy from us too?
- What brings you back to buy from us?
- What else could we be doing for you that we don't currently offer?
- How else can I help?

Review and revamp

Let's be honest. Customer feedback is great, but customers don't always know what they are talking about. At least that's how it can sometimes feel because you will find that only certain customers will be vocal enough to tell you what they think. Many of your customers who like what you do may be too shy to express their opinions; the customers who hate what you do will simply walk away without bothering to tell you why.

Never change everything you do solely on the basis of what your customers say, because they present you with only a particular view of what is working or not working in your business.

Instead, do your own analysis. Work your way through some of the following questions:

- What is popular and selling well? Why?
- Are there products or services that sell well at particular times of year, month, or day? What does that suggest you could change?
- What do you enjoy selling most? Are there any links between what you enjoy and what sells well or badly?
- What is selling poorly? Why?
- What would be the effect on the business of dropping whatever is selling poorly? Would anyone notice or care if you stopped selling those poorly performing offerings?

Conduct your own analysis and combine it with the ongoing feedback from your customers. Ask your team or confidants to throw their thoughts into the process too. Keep adjusting the mix of what you offer to move away from the less enjoyable and lower margin products and services. Figure out what you can improve or enhance, change or drop. Look for ways to avoid getting stuck in a rut.

Learn to let go

It's the end of yet another month and you have a clump of expenses to process, invoices to send out, bills to pay. My advice to you is not to do them; that's right, put them to one side because if you want to grow your business, you must learn to delegate – to pass less important work on to others and free yourself up to focus on the stuff that really matters.

It can be easy to get mired in your work, to see a long list of tasks and lose perspective of what counts – to think that if you don't do it, it won't get done. Even if you have yet to take on a single employee, look for ways to contract out tasks – whether it is menial work that sucks up your time or expert work that someone could do quicker and probably better. Hire an accountant or even a simple bookkeeper to handle your financial administration. Hand over whatever you can to caterers and lawyers, website designers and advisers.

Free yourself up to focus on marketing and networking, tweaking your business concept and selling to customers. Focus on the projects and tasks that make a material difference to your business and let other people take care of the rest.

Later on, when you have employees, don't think of what you can delegate so much as what you cannot delegate. Understand that lower-value activities must be done by lower-paid members of the team – even if you actually quite enjoy those activities – otherwise your business will not thrive. Make it your default option to delegate work unless it is something that absolutely, positively has to be done by you and you alone. Even if you know that no one else can do a job as perfectly and professionally as you, it doesn't matter so long as they do it well enough.

Instruct with intelligence

There's a big difference between delegating and dumping. Delegating is making sure someone feels comfortable with a task and ensuring that it will get done; dumping is throwing a task at a person and hoping that it gets done.

Effective delegation must answer the what, why, how, and when of a task. Whether you are briefing an external contractor or instructing one of your team, make sure that you:

- Explain what the task is, giving enough background so the person understands why it needs to be done. Focus on the positive consequences of success rather than what might happen if the person fails; the latter approach is a sure-fire way to demotivate others pretty damn quickly.
- Describe any important steps in how the task should be done, for example if the person could adopt an established method, ask for help from particular people, use a template, consult particular sources, and so on.
- Indicate exactly when the task needs to be completed by.

Use your judgment in deciding how much detail to provide. Just as there is a fine line between delegating and dumping, so too is there a thin divide between delegation (giving sufficient instruction for someone to do a task well) and patronization (giving so much instruction that a person feels that he or she is being treated like an idiot or dunce).

Over time, give others the opportunity to grow. Show that you trust them and allow them greater autonomy each time. Explain what needs doing but leave them to figure out how to do it.

Give effective feedback

Bosses hate it or forget to give it, but employees can't get enough of it. Yes, we're talking about feedback.

Your employees will get it wrong, hopefully not very often, but probably more often than you would like. In order to learn from their mistakes, employees must understand more about those mistakes.

Make sure the feedback you give is:

- Constructive. Make your feedback as palatable as possible by balancing the positive and the negative. Explain not only what went wrong but also what has gone right. Employees frequently complain that they typically only get feedback when things go wrong, and not enough recognition for when things go right. Even if someone does not get the results you were hoping for, you could still acknowledge the hard work they put into the task.
- Consistent. Aim to give feedback regularly to all members of the team. Be careful not to treat favorites

differently as it will damage the atmosphere within the team.

- Current. Give feedback sooner rather than later to ensure that the details are still fresh enough to discuss meaningfully. It also helps to prevent issues festering for too long.
- Candid. Of course be honest with your views, but likewise ask employees to be open in expressing their side of the story. If, for example, they feel that they were given poor instructions (by you), they need to be able to tell you without fear of reprisal.
- Clear. Check that the other person(s) understands how and why they went wrong. Perhaps ask them to explain back to you how they would do the task differently next time.

Once you have given feedback, move on. Don't bring it up again. People hate being beaten up repeatedly for the same mistake.

In my opinion, you would be stupid not to give feedback. It's the single biggest means in your toolkit for directing the behavior of the people who work for you. Oh, and don't forget to ask for feedback on your own performance occasionally too – it will stop you from turning into a rubbish boss.

Pay attention to relationships and tasks

Customers buy from businesses they like spending time with. If you are rude or overbearing with a customer you can wave them farewell, and the same is true for your employees too. Employees go out of their way to do well by bosses they like. If they do not like you – perhaps only respecting your knowledge but not warming to you on a personal level – they will only ever obey the precise instructions you give them. They will never go beyond the call of duty.

So bear this in mind as you go about directing and delegating to the members of your team. Work as much on building and maintaining excellent relationships with the members of the team as on making sure their work is good.

There may be times when you would be within your rights to pull people up about their shortcomings, to sit them down and give them feedback on why and how they went wrong. But, on occasion, it can pay dividends not to. Sometimes a knowing smile and a nod is all it takes to help people acknowledge their error, and, rather than beating them up endlessly about their mistake, it shows that you can be a magnanimous boss too.

Get to know the members of your team on a personal level. Encourage an atmosphere in which people feel able to talk about both their professional and personal worries rather than letting them stew and then boil over abruptly. Ask about their home lives and work concerns; listen to what is going on. Show that you can be both the boss and a human being who can understand and empathize with them. Show that you care and they will care about you and your business in return.

Cultivate your culture

How you behave sets an example for the people who work for you. What you say and do influences how others speak and behave.

Big organizations talk about their culture – the collection of attitudes, values, and implicit rules that govern how people behave towards customers and each other. Even if you are a small team, you would be wise to pay attention to the culture because everything you do and say has a multiplier effect. Others in the team will notice and use this as a template for how they should behave.

It's not just about the big stuff either. If you finish a phone call and laugh at how stupid a customer is, you make it acceptable for others to sneer at your customers behind their backs too. If you grumble about an employee to another member of the team rather than to the employee's face, you're communicating that it is acceptable for everyone to do that too. Tell a lie to a customer and you give license for everyone else to tell lies – even to you – too.

Be honest, own up to your mistakes and learn to back down and apologize when you are wrong. Turn up on time. Be realistic about what you can achieve and always follow through with your commitments. Behave towards your employees and customers exactly as you wish your employees to behave towards each other and your customers.

Invest in your business and people

When the business posts its first profits, crack open a bottle of Dom Pérignon, maybe get caterers to throw a party, celebrate but then take a moment to decide what to do with the profit.

The sensible entrepreneur will want to invest a significant chunk of the profit back into the business, using the cash to research and develop new products, update technology, and perhaps expand the size of the team. But investment should be about more than the business and its systems and processes and products. I've said it before and I shall say it again: Business is fundamentally about people, and your team has all played a part in making the business a success.

Be generous with whatever wealth you have generated. Steer clear of the temptation to hoard the profits. Too often entrepreneurs are depicted as sole warriors, soldiering on in the face of adversity and disbelief from others. However, the reality is that most entrepreneurs only succeed when they find the right people to help them on their journey.

Show your appreciation for the dedication of the team and spread the profits widely. It is far better to reward people well than have them decide that the success of the business no longer matters.

Create a board of advisers

Most large businesses have a professional board comprising executive and non-executive directors. In practice, executive directors tend to be involved in the day-to-day running of the business; non-executive directors tend to offer their advice on a less frequent basis on more strategic or critical decisions.

Hiring a board of directors may be a little excessive if you are still a small business, but the principle remains. Much as you sought a mentor to guide you through the earliest stages of your business, look now for further individuals to advise you and ensure that your business continues to grow and thrive.

Look for others you respect in business to act as your confidants. Ask them whether you can get together perhaps once every few months. If you cannot afford to pay them the market rate for their time, at least buy them a lavish dinner, or offer to trade your business's services. Tell them what you have been up to, your successes and struggles, about your key customers and troubles. Then listen. And listen well.

They may have a gem of a suggestion or two – the breakthrough ideas that catapult your business to the next level. Even if they do not tell you anything that you do not already know, they may remind you about some of the tasks that you have perhaps been putting off.

Your advisers need not be in the same industry as you. Depending on the issues you face, you might consider hiring an executive coach, a finance professional, a management consultant. Sometimes having someone look at your business from a new perspective could even be an advantage, giving you fresh insights that others within your own field might never have seen.

Make use of your advisers. Never be too proud to ask for and accept the advice of business-people you respect, because you know what they say about pride and falls.

Be a real person, not a business-person

Here's a quick challenge for you. Imagine you are networking and someone asks you what you do outside of work, as a hobby or for fun. What are you going to say?

Top entrepreneurs often juggle successful businesses with not only their home life but also sports or other interests and pursuits. They are balanced, rounded people who can entertain not only with stories of business travails but also personal endeavors.

Don't let your business become your sole focus to the exclusion of all else. Of course you need to work hard and will need to make sacrifices to turn your concept into a business. But you need to stay fresh. Just as sitting in front of a computer for hours on end dulls the senses and reduces your productivity, so too does spending too long thinking about nothing but work. No matter what else is going on, make it a priority to get out of the business. See friends, exercise, meditate, dine out, jab and box a punch bag, do charitable things, sculpt, watch a sports game, or whatever helps you to unwind.

This is not just about de-stressing. When you meet suppliers and customers, it helps to have something to talk about other than your work. Remember that people like people like themselves. If your customers and suppliers are normal people, they will have families, friends, and interests outside of their work. All work and no play makes you a very, very dull person indeed – the kind of slightly scary person that many people may decide they would rather not do business with.

Prepare to move on

True entrepreneurs are individuals who enjoy giving ideas form and substance, turning them into enterprises that can thrive in their own right. While entrepreneurs are usually good at starting up businesses, they are not always so good at running them.

If you decide to keep your business small (but growing professionally), you may be able to run the business forever. However, many entrepreneurs get bored with more of the same, of running a stable business day in and day out. Many get itchy feet and this can play havoc with an existing business because of their need to seek out new concepts and ideas to bring to market.

Even if you decide to grow your business, you may find that the running of a 50- or 100- or 200-person firm involves too much management, bureaucracy, and administration for your liking. You may miss the thrill of working in a tiny team, of generating ideas, selling, and being involved in every single decision.

So recognize when it is time for you to go.

Entrepreneurs do not always make good corporate managers. Of course you will be able to quote a dozen examples of entrepreneurs who are still heavily involved in the running of their business empires, but trust me, those are the exceptions to the rule.

Realize when it is time to hand over the top job. Invite a professional manager to head up the business. Sell your stake (and hopefully make lots of money out of it) and go and look for another way to set up a new business.

Depart with good grace, celebrate your momentous achievement and maybe take some time off. However, if you are like any of the truly notable entrepreneurs in the world, you probably won't be able to take much time off because you will be desperate to get back to working on your next "big idea"...

Final Thoughts

Several things are true of the entrepreneurial journey. Building your own business will be the most exciting, thrilling, and fulfilling work you can ever do. Yes, hard work and long hours are involved. Yes, so much can go wrong and it is your sole responsibility to make it go right. Get it right and you will create a business that you can be proud of, that will not only earn you a living, but also provide you with the lifestyle you aspire to. Pretty much anyone who becomes an entrepreneur would never go back to his/her old life.

Most important in the entrepreneurial journey is that the only person who can stop you from making it happen is you.

Entrepreneurs succeed because they are determined and are willing to invest long hours in bringing their dreams and ideas to market. They focus on their goals and do whatever it takes to make things happen. Remember to work smart rather than hard – to focus on the right work that makes a difference rather than work that merely makes you feel busy.

Often, the decisions you need to make are not difficult because they are hard to understand, so much as being hard to follow through with. When sales are slipping, you probably realize that you should get out but perhaps you don't want to because you enjoy delivering your product or service to existing customers more than pursuing new ones. Or when an employee continues to underperform despite your best efforts, you know that you will have to fire them, but again you keep putting it off because you don't want to have to do it.

Remember too that business is about people, people, people. Get out of your office and meet people, lots of people, and then go and meet some more. Connect with them, get them to like you, infect them with your vision, and engage them about the opportunities at hand. The more people you meet, the more likely you will come across great ideas, potential investors, new customers, the right suppliers, new employees.

If you need a bit of support in turning your goals into business success, why not email me at rob@talentspace. co.uk? In any case, I wish you success and happiness on your own personal entrepreneurial journey. Enjoy.

About the Author

Dr Rob Yeung is a director at business psychology consultancy Talentspace (www.talentspace.co.uk), where he specializes in psychological profiling and coaching on issues such as leadership and business growth. He has devised assessment centres and interviewed on behalf of organizations ranging from global investment banks, airlines, international law and accountancy firms to public sector organizations, media companies and start-up businesses. He has written a dozen books on career and management topics and often contributes to print media including the *Guardian* and *Financial Times* as well as broadcast media including CNN. A business school lecturer and frequently requested conference speaker, he is also the presenter of How To Get Your Dream Job, a highly acclaimed BBC television series on job hunting.

Books in the Business Solutions Series

EFFECTIVE DECISION MAKING
10 steps to better decision making and problem solving | Jeremy Kourdi

The very pressure for a decision often breeds indecisiveness This book enables you to find the best solutions and options, avoid pitfalls, manage risk, work with people to ensure that decisions succeed, and understand how you can improve the way you typically operate when making decisions.

BRILLIANT COMMUNICATION
5 steps to communicating your message clearly and effectively | Patrick Forsyth

Both written and presentational business communication are career skills in which one simply must excel. This book reviews the key factors that will help you prepare and communicate clearly, effectively and memorably.

THE NEW RULES OF ENTREPRENEURSHIP
What it really takes to become a savvy and successful entrepreneur | Rob Yeung

Combining genuinely practical advice with an easily digestible format, Rob Yeung guides you through the things you need to know in order to set up on your own business. This book shows you how to get motivated, make a business plan and sell your product quickly and effectively.

GREAT SELLING SKILLS
How to sell anything to anyone | Bob Etherington

Written in a quick-read and practical way, this book presents a set of simple, basic skills for selling, aimed exclusively at those people who have never been trained in the art of selling. Great Sellings Skills is intended to enable anyone to make a sound contribution to the overall sales process.

THE NEW RULES OF JOBHUNTING
A modern guide to finding the job you want | Rob Yeung

Job hunting is a job in itself. But too many books are aimed at helping career no-hopers get into a job – any job. This book is aimed at helping ambitious high fliers to, well, fly even higher. It will make sure you get the right job and maintain upward momentum in your career.

MANAGE YOUR BOSS
How to create the ideal working relationship | Patrick Forsyth

This book will enable you to create a relationship with your boss as something that can potentially help you do a good job and to meet specific job objectives. It also provides advice and tips on collaborating and working in parallel with your boss.

GREAT NEGOTIATING SKILLS
The essential guide to getting what you want | Bob Etherington
This book is packed with anecdotes and advice for all those people who are generally terrible at negotiating and would like to do it better.

SURVIVING OFFICE POLITICS
Coping and succeeding in the workplace jungle | Patrick Forsyth
Office politics happens – whether you want to admit it or not. But politicking need not always be bad. Here is the definitive answer to engaging with office politics to further your own career in a positive fashion– and deal with the Machiavellian types and pre-empt their efforts.